Sentence Combining
Shaping Ideas for Better Style

Sentence Combining
Shaping Ideas for Better Style

John Clifford
Robert F. Waterhouse

Bobbs-Merrill Educational Publishing
Indianapolis

Developed for Bobbs-Merrill Educational Publishing
by Visual Education Corporation

Sponsoring Editor: James B. Smith
Project Editor: Mark Schaeffer
Production Manager: Gary F. Pugh

The Bobbs-Merrill Company, Inc.
4300 West 62nd Street
Indianapolis, Indiana 46268

First Edition
First Printing 1983

Library of Congress Cataloging in Publication Data

Clifford, John.
  Sentence combining.

  1. English language—Rhetoric. I. Waterhouse,
  Robert F., 1941–   . II. Title.
  PE1408.C529 1983   808'.042   82-22803
  ISBN 0-672-61605-X

Contents

Preface

Sentence Combining: Shaping Ideas for Better Style has been put together in the conviction that sentence combining is extremely valuable for helping writers develop flexibility with language, and that it still has not developed its full potential. The technique is increasingly used at the college as well as at the high school level, and it has been validated by positive findings in several studies. Nevertheless, sentence combining is rarely integrated into the main flow of composition classes: it has tended to be a sideshow, albeit a valuable one, rather than a part of the three-ring circus itself. The three-ring circus in question, of course, is defined by the three major steps commonly conceptualized in the writing process —generating ideas through research, free writing, and other techniques; constructing a first draft by organizing and developing these ideas; and editing to a polished version by evaluating and refining what one has written.

Sentence combining is commonly viewed, like grammar, as a technique to supply students with skills needed for the writing process. Indeed, it is often seen as a painless alternative to grammar itself, an alternative that can lead students to produce, by example and practice, sentences which they are unable to produce by analysis and prescriptive rules. Thus, like grammar, it is thought of as supplementary to the main drive of the composition course, which is to teach students to express and structure their ideas more effectively.

Our own view is different. Sentence combining, we believe, provides a unique and necessary contribution to the writing class that cannot be provided by grammar. It demonstrates, as no other technique can, the great versatility and flexibility of language; and it shows how this flexibility can be applied throughout the process of composition to shape and reshape ideas.

Open sentence-combining exercises—in which students are asked to work on a sequence of sentences without guidance from specific cues or models—can be thought of as requiring three separate abilities from the student, each one related to the flexibility of language. First comes the ability to reshape a simple sentence in a number of different ways—as other sentences, or as phrases that can be incorporated into longer sentences. Second comes the ability to organize and combine these elements into a piece of writing that works. And third is the ability to evaluate the result and to consider whether alternative combinations might not be superior from the point of view of style or meaning. At every stage, the student experiences the flexibility of language. The student can realize that an idea once expressed is not cast in stone, but can be manipulated and reshaped for better effect.

The parallels between these three abilities and the three steps of the writing process should be clear. Prewriting can encompass a very involved set of techniques; but it does include producing, manipulating and noting down the simple elements from which a composition will be constructed. Writing involves shaping these elements into a working piece of prose. And editing is a continual process of breaking down and restructuring for the sake of more effective expression.

Sentence Combining: Shaping Ideas for Better Style presents 44 open sentence-combining exercises in which students may experiment with and practice the flexibility of language. It also contains exercises designed to give directed practice with each of the abilities described. Part One includes 5 exercises where students rearrange, or transform, simple idea sentences into a variety of different shapes. Part Two contains 30 exercises which involve combining simple idea sentences into a variety of more complex expressions. And Part Three offers 8 exercises in which students take complex sentences, break them down into simple elements, and recombine them for better effect.

Although these directed exercises are of three different types, they all follow the same basic strategy: they lead students to develop not one answer, but three or four alternative answers, and then select the most appropriate one to fit a given context. We have informally called these exercises "multiple modeled" exercises. Students consider a model that shows several expressions derived from a given sentence or set of sentences; then they follow the model and produce similar sets of expressions from other given sentences.

Such exercises are based on the simple modeled exercises that are commonly used in other sentence-combining texts. We have felt that simple modeled exercises strongly imply that there is only one correct way to combine a given set of sentences—an implication not fully countered even when the accompanying text states that other combinations are possible. Therefore, we have made the flexibility of language explicit by providing multiple models—and inviting students to generate additional versions of their own if they can.

The *content* of the exercises in this book, both the modeled and the open ones, is wide-ranging. We have shown language being used for a variety of different subjects in a variety of different disciplines, in order to encourage students to generalize their learning to writing in those other disciplines. The topics selected are intended to be eye-catching and interesting, so that students will not fall into the trap of doing the exercises by rote; instead they will be aware of the ideas they are expressing. We have included occasional exercises where the topic is undefined, so that students can work with their own ideas, but in general we have avoided fantasy and invention and tried to stick to interesting, concrete facts.

The *organization* of the book within its three parts has been dictated more by meaning relationships than by grammar. In other words, we do have a set of exercises on phrases, followed by a set of exercises on clauses. Instead, we use headings such as "Description" and "Causality," focusing on the purpose of the construction used. This format is consistent with recent linguistic theory, which is increasingly reluctant to describe language without reference to meaning. It also seems consistent with our intuitive sense of what writers do.

Writing itself starts with intention and meaning, not grammar. The writer does not think "I want to use a clause," but rather "I want to describe something." This intention may translate into several different grammatical forms—an adjective, a descriptive phrase, an adjectival clause. Similarly, writers who want to describe an action may use a verb or noun depending on the context. It is the purpose, not the part of speech, that is primary. For this reason we have minimized the role of grammar in the book, excluding it from the organization and using the terminology very infrequently.

Grammar, as a tool of analysis and prescription, is on a high level of abstraction. It is more advanced and difficult than the work we are providing here. While we were obviously concerned with remaining consistent with grammatical formulations, this book can be used independently of grammatical knowledge: it is designed to help develop an intuitive understanding of language flexibility. For this purpose it has avoided using the signal systems often used in sentence-combining exercises; and it has also striven to provide sentence sequences that sound natural—even if this means they must be slightly longer than the ideal "kernel" sentence.

A book of this length cannot hope to be exhaustive in its coverage of language, and we do not pretend that it is. Its purpose is not to give students practice at all the subtleties of language—that would be impossible in a book twenty times its length. It merely seeks to give them enough exposure to sentence flexibility to realize that flexibility is a major feature of language that can be mastered and used in writing. Students who work through this book will build a feeling for the flexibility of language and be more able to express their ideas in a number of different ways.

Needless to say, we owe a considerable debt to many people for this book. The theorists of transformational grammar have provided the formal insights on which the practice of sentence combining is based. The pioneers in the field, Francis Christensen and

Kellogg Hunt, have helped to establish the technique. Other authors in the field have furthered the theory and practice of sentence combining, providing a background for this particular book.

In addition, we have benefited from the valuable advice of William Smith, at Utah State University, and Elisabeth McPherson, formerly at Lake Forest Community College. Without their critical comments, this book would be very much less than it is.

Finally, our thanks are due to Holly Hughes, Barbara McHale, Georgella Moncrief, Janet Powell, Charlotte Solomon, Sheera Stern, Susan Sweet, Barbara Uittenbogaard, and Erich Woiset·schlaeger, who all helped to construct the exercises; to Cynthia Feldner, who has labored long over this manuscript with a recalci· trant word processor; and to Mark Schaeffer, without whose tireless work this book could never have seen the light of day.

John Clifford
Bob Waterhouse

Sentence Combining
Shaping Ideas for Better Style

PART ONE:
ARRANGING

INTRODUCTION

Writing is as much a part of the life of a college student as eating, speaking, or breathing. In the course of a single day, you might be called upon to prepare a lab report for a science course, send a thank-you note to a friend, compose a cover letter to accompany a job application, and write a two-page essay on an English exam. Because each of these activities is so different from the others, you probably don't group them together in your mind. Nevertheless, a little reflection will tell you that all of these types of writing have two important things in common.

First, a piece of writing—*any* piece of writing—has a **purpose.** You, the writer, have some information that you want to communicate to someone else. That information may consist of facts, opinions, feelings, observations, or any combination of these. Whether you are writing an essay, a report, a letter, or even a story, the purpose of your writing is to make your information understandable to another person.

Second, a piece of writing has a **style.** Style has less to do with what is said than with *how* it is said. In our discussion, the word **style** will be used very loosely: the length of your sentences, the way you order and arrange your thoughts, and even the way your words sound to the reader will all be considered matters of style. While the purpose of a piece of writing is usually fixed from the start, the style may change several times from the time you begin writing to the time you finish.

Style is most often associated with clothing, and its meaning in that context is not very different. Nearly all clothing, after all, has the same purpose: to cover you and to keep you warm. As you've surely discovered, however, wearing clothing of the wrong style can be almost as bad as wearing no clothing at all. When you dress, you ask yourself many questions: "Does my clothing suit me? Is it appropriate for the occasion? Does my sweater match my shirt? Is my outfit fashionable enough? Is it *too* fashionable? What will this outfit say about me?"

When you write, you should be asking yourself similar questions. "Does my writing style suit the subject matter? Is it appropriate for the occasion? Do my sentences sound good together? Is my writing sophisticated enough? Is it *too* sophisticated? What will this piece of writing say about *me*?"

People who have had a lot of practice in selecting clothing are aware of some helpful tricks. They know, for instance, that vertical stripes can make them look thinner and that horizontal stripes can make them look heavier. Similarly, experienced writers know how to arrange sentences in a way that will produce the effect they want. For example, consider these two sentences:

1.   Wolves rarely attack humans.
2.   Humans are rarely attacked by wolves.

You'll notice that both sentences say exactly the same thing—but the first sentence seems to say something about wolves, while the second seems to say something about humans. Both sentences serve the same *purpose,* but they are written in slightly different *styles.*

Just as the experienced clothes-wearer knows which of two similar shirts will look best in a specific situation, the experienced writer can decide which of these two sentences to use in a specific context. If you were writing an essay about wolves, for example, you might begin with the following paragraph:

If you hear a nearby howl in the night, you have very little to fear. _____; when they are, it is nearly always because the wolf is rabid. Healthy wolves prefer smaller prey, such as mice and squirrels.

Which of the two sentence examples would you use to fill in the blank? Let's try each one in turn and see how they work.

1.   If you hear a nearby howl in the night, you have very little to fear. **Wolves rarely attack humans;** when they are, it is nearly always because the wolf is rabid. Healthy wolves prefer smaller prey, such as mice and squirrels.
2.   If you hear a nearby howl in the night, you have very little to fear. **Humans are rarely attacked by wolves;** when they are, it is nearly always because the wolf is rabid. Healthy wolves prefer smaller prey, such as mice and squirrels.

The choice in this case is easy, since only one of the two sentences makes sense when it is inserted in the blank. Using sentence 1 in this paragraph causes an obvious problem: the phrase that follows it, **when they are,** doesn't seem to mean anything. (The reader would tend to ask, "When *who* are *what?*") On the other hand, using sentence 2 solves that problem neatly: **when they are** now clearly means **when humans are attacked.**

Let's say, however, that your essay about wolves began somewhat differently. Which of the two sentence examples would you use in *this* case?

> The fairy tale "Little Red Riding Hood" has given wolves an unde-servedly bad reputation. _____and certainly never eat them.

Once again, we try each one and see how they work:

1. The fairy tale "Little Red Riding Hood" has given wolves an undeservedly bad reputation. **Wolves rarely attack humans** and certainly never eat them.
2. The fairy tale "Little Red Riding Hood" has given wolves an undeservedly bad reputation. **Humans are rarely attacked by wolves** and certainly never eat them.

Here we run into an interesting problem. Both versions of the paragraph make sense, but they seem to say different things. The first version seems to talk about wolves that eat people, while the second seems to talk about people who eat wolves. You probably decided that sentence 1 works better in the paragraph, but how did you make that decision?

First of all, you're probably familiar with the story of "Little Red Riding Hood." You know that the wolf in the story eats Red Riding Hood's grandmother and threatens to eat Red for dessert—certainly a case of wolves eating people and not the other way around. But even if you didn't know the story, you could still have found another clue in the paragraph: " . . . has given wolves an undeservedly bad reputation." You could logically conclude from this that the paragraph is about something bad that wolves (*not* humans) are reputed to do. In either case, you are using your own knowledge and judgment to make the choice.

For a final example of this decision-making process, let's imagine that your essay on wolves included the following paragraph:

> In the winter, when food is scarce, wolves roam in large hunting packs. A wolf pack may go after a lamb or a calf, but _____
> _____.

Which of the two sentence examples would you use to complete this paragraph? Let's look at each one:

1. In the winter, when food is scarce, wolves roam in large hunting packs. A wolf pack may go after a lamb or calf, but **wolves rarely attack humans.**
2. In the winter, when food is scarce, wolves roam in large hunting packs. A wolf pack may go after a lamb or calf, but **humans are rarely attacked by wolves.**

The choice here is much more difficult: *both* versions of the paragraph seem to work. No matter which sentence is put in the blank, the paragraph makes sense and keeps the same meaning. Yet you, the writer, are forced to choose one or the other. (If not, you'll never finish your essay.) How do you decide?

When nothing else makes a difference, there is always one question left that you can ask yourself: "Which version *sounds* better?" To answer that question, you may even try reading the paragraph out loud. Which version is more comfortable to read? In which version do the stresses and pauses fall more naturally? In which version does the meaning seem clearer? Surprisingly, most experienced writers tend to agree on decisions like these. You'll probably find, in the above example, that you and your classmates will tend to choose version 1 over version 2.

If you disagree—if your "ear" tells you that the second version is better than the first, or if you honestly don't hear any difference between them—don't despair. The exercises in this book will give you extensive practice in making decisions like these, and you'll soon find that your judgment agrees more and more with that of your classmates and your instructor. More important, however, is the fact that many stylistic decisions are neither "right" nor "wrong." Even professional writers disagree with each other, in many cases, about what sounds better than what. We have, as a result, many different writing styles to choose from—and yours will always be completely your own.

PREWRITING

Every writer knows that the hardest part of writing is getting started. You have almost certainly encountered this problem yourself if you have had to write a term paper. With pen in hand, you stare at a blank piece of paper for what seems like hours. You roll ideas around in your mind, perhaps make a few notes, and search for a place to start. You may write a couple of sentences or paragraphs, then cross them out. You may begin again, then stop to organize a few more notes. You may even crumple up your first sheet of paper in disgust. Finally, after a few more attempts, you hit upon an opening sentence that seems to work, and your ideas begin to flow more clearly and logically.

This trial-and-error method is really not far from what most professional writers do. However, they have probably made their approach a little more systematic over the years. They may have one method that they prefer to start with—for example, writing a few spontaneous pages without being too critical of the result, or keeping a list of thoughts that they have about the topic, or perhaps discussing the idea with a group of friends and making notes after the session. If they find that their first strategy is unproductive—and writing is always full of false starts—then they'll switch their strategy and try their second-favorite method. In some cases, writers must try three or four different strategies before they are satisfied with the direction their writing has taken.

In composition classes, you may well be given advice on a set of strategies to follow for your own writing. This advice will put you a step ahead of the term paper writer two paragraphs back: you will have a systematic method of teasing ideas out of your mind and onto the page. With further experience, you will be able to adapt the system you've learned so that it works best for your own particular mind—and then you'll be on your way to becoming a fluent writer.

This book is not meant to teach you how to find ideas, organize your thoughts, or develop a formal outline—these things are better learned from a rhetoric or writing handbook. However, at some point during the process of discovering and shaping your thoughts (the phase often called *prewriting*), you will develop a set of sentences or notes that you want to meld into a continuous piece of writing. It is at this point that the exercises in this book start to be useful. They may not resemble anything you will ever encounter in your own writing—although they may occasionally come close—but they will help you to develop flexibility in the way you express yourself on paper. You'll learn how to use a variety of sentence styles that both sound good and can do justice to your ideas.

Every writer has experienced the problem of getting attached to a particular way of expressing an idea. It seems to sound more natural in a certain sequence of words. (Often, this is the form in which the writer first expressed the idea or got it onto paper.) The mark of seasoned writers, however, is that they are willing to reshape any part of their work—including individual sentences—for the sake of the whole. And this willingness involves being able to think of a number of different expressions for the same idea—being, in other words, a flexible user of language.

You probably can already use language flexibly. You often express ideas differently in different situations. For example, consider these sentences:

1. I want you to finish this before you leave today.
2. Would you finish this before you leave today?
3. Finish this before you leave today!

These three sentences might all be used for the same purpose, but they would probably be used under quite different circumstances. For instance, which version would you use if you were talking to your boss, or to your professor? (Most people would agree that version 2 is the most appropriate.)

No idea has only one sequence of words that will express it. The English language is extremely versatile, and it allows a surprising number of possibilities. Some choices, as in the preceding example, may be influenced by the audience you are addressing, and may thus be related to your *purpose.* You made the selection you did as a result of your ideas about good manners and about how you can best influence people. Many more choices are made on the basis of *style.* In these cases, you select the sequence of words that will best fit in with the rest of what you are trying to say.

The easiest choice is usually not the best choice. If, for instance, you express all of your ideas in short, simple sentences, you may think you have expressed your ideas adequately. But this is not necessarily so—in fact, it is extremely unlikely. For a start, simple sentences are nearly always monotonous and dull—there is little variation in sentence length to involve the reader in your thoughts. If you can join some of the sentences into longer ones, you will be able to vary the pace and keep your audience more interested. In addition, simple sentences may be repetitious and misleading. Certain words may be repeated many times if you did not use words like **it** and **them** (pronouns) to avoid the repetition. Even if you did use pronouns, it may not be clear what they refer to. Only by choosing an appropriate form for expressing your ideas can you be sure that the reader will understand what you mean.

This concern with using language flexibly is an essential part of getting your ideas ready for an essay. If you become too attached to the way you express these ideas the first time around, you may never succeed in doing them full justice. The exercises in this book will make you more aware of the number of possibilities open to you, so that your fragmentary notes and opening sentences can be put together into a working whole.

COMBINING

An unbroken series of simple sentences is dull.
It is boring.
It is often difficult to read.

There is an explanation for this.
People have learned to expect variety.
They expect it in every aspect of their lives.
They like to eat different types of food.
They like to wear different types of clothing.
They like to read different types of sentences.
(They like different types of sentences as much as anything else.)

As you can see from the preceding paragraph, a list of simple sentences is far from a finished piece of writing. The rest of this book will show you an assortment of techniques that you can use to make your writing more cohesive, readable, and polished. We'll be starting with simple sentences like the ones above and putting them together in a number of different and interesting ways.

Even without sophisticated tricks, however, you can make simple sentences more readable simply by linking them together. Here's how the opening paragraph of this section might have looked if we'd added a few **ands** and replaced some periods with commas, semicolons, and colons:

VERSION 1:
An unbroken series of simple sentences is dull; it is boring; and it is often difficult to read. There is an explanation for this: people have learned to expect variety. They expect it in every aspect of their lives. They like to eat different types of food; they like to wear different types of clothing; and they like to read different types of sentences. (They like different types of sentences as much as anything else.)

You can see that even minor changes in structure and punctuation can make a paragraph sound better. By combining sentences in a more complicated way, and by eliminating some repetitive and unnecessary words, we can make the paragraph even more readable:

VERSION 2:
An unbroken series of simple sentences is dull, boring, and often difficult to read. The explanation is that people have learned to expect variety in every aspect of their lives. They like to eat different types of food, wear different types of clothing, and (as much as anything else) read different types of sentences.

Of course, as we discussed in the Introduction, there is no one "right" style for any piece of writing. Here is how another writer might combine the same set of sentences into a paragraph:

VERSION 3:
Apart from being dull and boring, an unbroken series of simple sentences is often difficult to read. Why? Because people have learned to expect variety in every aspect of their lives. They like to read different types of sentences as much as they like to eat different types of food or wear different types of clothing.

You'll notice that all three versions of this paragraph say the same thing—they just say it in different ways. (Other versions of the paragraph are also possible, of course; you may want to try one of your own just for practice.) Deciding which version is best in a particular context is simply a matter of judgment. As we mentioned before, it often helps to consider the *sound* of a piece of writing. Most people would feel, for instance, that version 3 of the opening paragraph sounds more impatient and aggressive than version 2. Since this book is intended to be patient and friendly, we probably would have chosen version 2 to open the section.

Before we begin to explore specific techniques for sentence arranging and combining, it's a good idea for you to try to do some on your own. Open Exercises A and B will give you a chance to test your judgment and to get your "ear" in gear. Feel free to experiment, but remember that even minor changes can make a big difference.

OPEN EXERCISE A

The following simple sentences constitute a short essay called "Remember This." Rewrite the sentences as a series of paragraphs. (A gap between lines indicates where a new paragraph should begin.) Remember that you can change punctuation, eliminate unnecessary words, and combine simple sentences in order to form more complex sentences. Keep in mind that there is no single "correct" answer. Compare your finished essay with those of your classmates and be prepared to discuss the choices you have made.

1. Why is it easy to remember the words of a favorite song?

2.   Why is it harder to remember the facts for an important test?
3.   Why do people remember some things?
4.   Why do people forget other things?
5.   Memories are very important to people.
6.   This is why psychologists have asked these questions.
7.   They have asked other questions as well.
8.   Their questions are about the processes of memory.

9.   Various factors contribute to people's forgetfulness.
10.   One factor is the passage of time.
11.   This factor is one of the most important.
12.   As more time passes, people forget more information.
13.   This is understandable.
14.   Another factor is the number of events that occur in time.
15.   People may learn something.
16.   They may experience events afterward.
17.   Experiencing many events will have a result.
18.   The result is that people forget more of what they learned.
19.   This is why people forget less while they are asleep.
20.   They forget more while they are awake.
21.   Fewer events happen during sleep.
22.   Events can interfere with people's remembering.
23.   There still is another factor.
24.   It is the similarity of the things being learned.
25.   For example, people can learn to rollerskate.
26.   They can then learn a telephone number.
27.   Learning the first does not interfere with learning the second.
28.   This is because the two activities are different.

29.   There is a method for improving memory.
30.   This method uses various devices and associations.
31.   The method is called mnemonics.
32.   One mnemonic device is to put information into a rhyme.
33.   Such information can be more easily remembered.
34.   This is why words to a song are remembered easily.
35.   A list of state capitals is remembered less easily.
36.   There are other methods to improve memory.
37.   One is to review the information frequently.
38.   Another is to recite the information while learning it.
39.   Still another is to devise cues.

40. These cues will help in retrieving the information.
41. You may be able to remember these techniques.
42. Then you will be able to remember other things as well.

OPEN EXERCISE B

The following simple sentences constitute a short essay called "The Uncrowned King." Rewrite the sentences as a series of paragraphs. (A gap between lines indicates where a new paragraph should begin.) Remember that you can change punctuation, eliminate unnecessary words, and combine simple sentences in order to form more complex sentences. Keep in mind that there is no single "correct" answer. Compare your finished essay with those of your classmates and be prepared to discuss the choices you have made.

1. Ireland struggled for nearly 700 years.
2. The struggle was for independence from England.
3. England was Ireland's neighbor.
4. England was powerful.
5. Charles Stewart Parnell led the Irish people during the 1880s.
6. He led them in their fight for freedom.
7. Parnell's support for the Irish cause was surprising.
8. Nevertheless, Parnell became a strong leader.
9. He was known as "The Uncrowned King of Ireland."

10. Parnell's support for the Irish cause surprised people.
11. This is because he was a wealthy landowner.
12. Most wealthy Irish landowners favored English rule in Ireland.
13. Parnell's decision was influenced by his mother.
14. His mother was an American.
15. She was anti-English.
16. Parnell had some unpleasant experiences.
17. These experiences were at school at Oxford.
18. These experiences also turned him against the English.

19. Parnell had a striking appearance.
20. He had a thick black beard.
21. He also had a stately bearing.
22. His appearance helped him.

23. He became a representative at the English Parliament.
24. The English Parliament met in Westminster.
25. There he led the struggle for Home Rule.
26. Home Rule was a right that the Irish people wanted.
27. It was the right to decide their own internal affairs.
28. He had almost reached his goal.
29. Then personal misfortune brought about his fall.
30. His misfortune also brought the failure of the Irish cause.

31. Parnell had loved Kitty O'Shea.
32. He had loved her for years.
33. She was the wife of one of his followers.
34. This follower was in the Irish party.
35. His name was Captain O'Shea.
36. Captain O'Shea sued for divorce.
37. This caused a scandal.
38. The scandal caused a terrible split.
39. The split was inside and outside the party.
40. All Ireland was divided.
41. The division was between Parnellites and anti-Parnellites.
42. Parnell struggled to keep his power.
43. He became ill and died in the struggle.
44. His death left Ireland in a more forlorn state than ever.

SENTENCE FLEXIBILITY

Combining sentences becomes easier when you are able to make stylistic changes in the sentences themselves. You already saw one example of this in the Introduction: **Wolves rarely attack humans** became **Humans are rarely attacked by wolves.** There was no change in the meaning of the sentence, but there *was* a change in emphasis: the first sentence seemed to have more to do with wolves, while the second seemed to have more to do with humans. A similar change can produce a sentence that puts the emphasis on the attack: **An attack by wolves on humans is rare.** (Here, interestingly, the stress seems to be more on humans than on wolves—even though the word **humans** comes later in the sentence. We can change this, however, with still another sentence arrangement: **An attack on humans by wolves is rare.**)

As you can see, even very simple sentences are immensely flexible. We can increase that flexibility still further by changing sentences into non-sentences—or, more specifically, into *phrases.* A sentence, as you probably know, can stand on its own, whereas a phrase cannot. We'll indicate that an arrangement of words is a phrase by adding three dots (...) to its beginning or end. These dots show how the phrase might fit into a sentence.

You'll find out how useful phrases can be if you try to move **rare(ly)** to the front of our sentence about wolves. **Rarely, wolves attack humans** seems awkward; **[Only] rarely do wolves attack humans** sounds formal and somewhat stilted. Shakespeare might have been able to say **Rare is an attack on humans by wolves,** but *you'll* never get away with it. You can, however, transform the sentence into some useful phrases beginning with **rare(ly):**

1. Rare attacks on humans by wolves ...
2. The rarity of an attack on humans by wolves ...

Several more phrases, which don't begin with **rare(ly),** are also possible:

3. Wolves, which rarely attack humans ...
4. Humans, who are rarely attacked by wolves ...
5. Attacks by wolves on humans, rare as they are ...

Later, when you begin to combine sentences, you can use phrases such as these as parts of longer, more complex sentences:

1. Records of North American naturalists reveal only **rare attacks on humans by wolves,** and none of these has been scientifically verified.
3. **Wolves, which rarely attack humans,** are nevertheless being exterminated by fearful hunters and trappers.
5. **Attacks by wolves on humans, rare as they are,** have somehow become a major part of our mythology—most recently in stories and films involving vampires.

Whether you are turning sentences into phrases or simply rearranging them to change their emphasis, you should always keep one principle in mind: the *meaning* of a sentence must not be changed by your transformations. You can, for instance, change **The food Napoleon ate was poisoned** to **Napoleon ate poisoned food**—but you cannot, under any circumstances, change it to **Poisoned food ate Napoleon.** The English language offers us a good deal of freedom, but to abuse this freedom is to put yourself in danger of being eaten by your dinner.

SENTENCE ARRANGING

We could easily talk for several more chapters about the flexibility of language—but you would probably learn very little. Rearranging sentences is, after all, a bit like juggling: it's fun to watch someone else do it, but it takes a good deal of practice before you can do it yourself. You'll find that, from this point on, this book is made up mostly of exercises. Once you become accustomed to the way these exercises work, you'll be on the road to becoming an expert juggler of words.

The type of exercise you'll encounter most often in this book is the so-called "modeled" exercise. In general, this means that the exercise will begin by showing you a model of how a sentence (or group of sentences) might be changed. You'll then be asked to "follow the model" by changing other sentences in exactly the same way. The types of models you are given will change throughout the book, but your task—to examine the model carefully and then imitate it—will stay basically the same.

Let's look closely at the type of modeled exercise you'll be working with in this part of the book. Since we've been talking most recently about rearranging sentences, each new model will show you several different ways in which a single sentence might be changed. One model, for example, might look like this:

IDEA ARRANGEMENTS:
(a) Wolves rarely attack humans.
(b) Humans are rarely attacked by wolves.
(c) An attack by wolves on humans is rare.

(d) The rarity of an attack on humans by wolves . . .

The first thing you'll be asked to do is to decide which arrangement works best in a particular context. For example:

Select the arrangement that works best in the following context.

CONTEXT:
The fairy tale "Little Red Riding Hood" has given wolves an unde-servedly bad reputation. _____and certainly never eat them.

As you'll remember from our earlier discussion, the correct answer here is (a). (There won't always be one "correct" answer, but be prepared to explain why you chose the answer you did.) If you have trouble with this part of the exercise, you may want to review pages 4–6.

Now comes the part of the exercise where you are asked to imitate the model. You'll be asked to do this several times in several sections of the exercise; each new section is indicated by a number. The first section might look like this:

Now create similar arrangements for the following ideas. On line e, add your own arrangement. Then select the one that best fits the given context.

1

IDEA ARRANGEMENTS:
(a) Buddhist monks customarily wear yellow robes.
(b) _____
(c) _____
(d) _____
(e) _____

CONTEXT:
_____and can be traced back to the fourth century B.C.

In order to work this section of the exercise, you have to look back to the model. Arrangement (b) of the model, for instance, brings

humans up to the front of the sentence; you know, therefore, that you will have to bring **yellow robes** to the front of the sentence you're now working with:

> Humans are rarely attacked by wolves.
> Yellow robes are customarily worn by Buddhist monks.

Similarly, arrangement (c) of the model brings **attack** to the front of the sentence and changes it to a noun; you'll have to do the same thing with **wear.** (Notice, too, how the adverb **customarily** becomes the adjective **customary**—just as **rarely** becomes **rare**):

> An attack by wolves on humans is rare.
> The wearing of yellow robes by Buddhist monks is customary.

Finally, arrangement (d) of the model changes the sentence into a phrase that begins with **the rarity** (the noun form of **rarely**). You, therefore, will have to change the new sentence into a phrase that begins with a noun form of **customarily:**

> The rarity of an attack on humans by wolves ...
> The custom of wearing yellow robes by Buddhist monks ...

The full solution, then, would look like this:

(a) Buddhist monks customarily wear yellow robes.
(b) Yellow robes are customarily worn by Buddhist monks.
(c) The wearing of yellow robes by Buddhist monks is customary.
(d) The custom of wearing yellow robes by Buddhist monks ...

You still have two more things to do before you go on to the next section of the exercise. First, you are asked to fill in line e with your own arrangement. The choice here is completely yours—you can add another sentence variation (such as **It is the custom of Buddhist monks to wear yellow robes**) or you can transform the sentence into a phrase (such as **Buddhist monks, who customarily wear yellow robes ...**). In some cases, you should be able to invent a combination that works even better than the ones in the model. Next, you are asked which of the combinations fits best in the given context. If you try each one in turn, you'll discover that both (b) and (c) make sense when inserted in the blank:

(b) Yellow robes are customarily worn by Buddhist monks and can be traced back to the fourth century B.C.
(c) The wearing of yellow robes by Buddhist monks is customary and can be traced back to the fourth century B.C.

Version (b), however, is somewhat ambiguous: is it *yellow robes* that date back to 400 B.C., or the monks' custom of *wearing* them? The best solution would have to be (c), since this version can clearly be interpreted only one way. On the other hand, your own version (e) may work even better than (c).

Following this section of the exercise comes another numbered section that refers to the *same model*. Here, however, a different arrangement might be supplied:

2

IDEA ARRANGEMENTS:
(a) _____
(b) _____
(c) _____
(d) The bravery of Nathan Hale's acceptance of death . . .
(e) _____

CONTEXT:
_____, but his last words were not so poetic as those that are usually ascribed to him. What he actually said was, "It is the duty of every good officer to obey any orders given him by his commander-in-chief."

By looking back at the **Wolves rarely attack humans** model, you can arrive at the following solution:

(a) Nathan Hale bravely accepted death.
(b) Death was bravely accepted by Nathan Hale.
(c) The acceptance of death by Nathan Hale was brave.
(d) The bravery of Nathan Hale's acceptance of death . . .

(e) [Your choice]

When you then try each arrangement in the supplied context, you'll discover that (a), (b), and (c) all make sense. Version (a), however, produces the clearest, best-*sounding* sentence. Most people would agree, in this case, that (a) is the best answer—unless, of course, your own version (e) is better.

Each modeled exercise includes four numbered sections like these, and each section refers back to the same model. Every time you begin a *new* modeled exercise, you'll be working with an entirely different model—and you'll have another chance to find out firsthand just how flexible the English language can be.

Please note: This is not a workbook. The blank lines in the exercises are for illustration only; they are not intended to be written on. Do all your work on a separate sheet of paper. Don't write in the book.

When you've finished the five modeled exercises that follow, you'll have another chance to try your hand at some "open" exercises. These are lists of simple sentences that need to be rewritten as essays, and they're just like the exercises you did earlier in the book. Now, however, you have a few more tricks up your sleeve, and the finished essays that come out of these later exercises will probably be even more interesting and varied. Completing all of these exercises—"modeled" and "open"—will prepare you for the more sophisticated sentence combining techniques we'll be working with in Part Two.

MODELED EXERCISE A

IDEA ARRANGEMENTS:
(a) President Ford vetoed bills frequently.
(b) Bills were frequently vetoed by President Ford.
(c) The vetoing of bills by President Ford was frequent.
(d) The frequency with which President Ford vetoed bills . . .

Select the arrangement that works best in the following context.

CONTEXT:
More bills were rejected by Gerald Ford than by any other American president. _____led some observers to worry that he was thwarting the wishes of Congress.

Now create similar arrangements for the following ideas. On line e, add your own arrangement. Then select the one that best fits the given context.

1

IDEA ARRANGEMENTS:
(a) The ancient Greeks predicted eclipses of the sun accurately.
(b) _____
(c) _____
(d) _____
(e) _____

CONTEXT:
_____, who discovered they occurred every 18 years and 17 days.

2

IDEA ARRANGEMENTS:
(a) _____
(b) _____
(c) The reporting of facts by journalists is objective.
(d) _____
(e) _____

CONTEXT:
_____is always questioned, but recently, landmark damage suits against writers have forced them to tighten their own standards of proof.

3

IDEA ARRANGEMENTS:
(a) _____
(b) _____
(c) _____
(d) The vividness with which the northern lights illuminate the Alaskan sky . . .
(e) _____

CONTEXT:
_____but are never seen in the Soviet Union. Scientists believe the lights, known as the aurora borealis, are caused by the effects of sunspot activity on the earth's magnetic field.

4

IDEA ARRANGEMENTS:

(a) _____

(b) _____

(c) The shrinkage of the money supply by high interest rates is rapid.

(d) _____

(e) _____

CONTEXT:

_____was demonstrated in 1978. Tight money policies caused an immediate decrease in the rate of inflation, but an increase in unemployment.

MODELED EXERCISE B

IDEA ARRANGEMENTS:

(a) Squirrels compulsively store food.

(b) Food is compulsively stored by squirrels.

(c) The compulsive storage of food by squirrels . . .

(d) The compulsiveness with which squirrels store food . . .

Select the arrangement that works best in the following context.

CONTEXT:

_____often leads to excessive hoarding. A squirrel may hide ten times as much as it can possibly use in one winter.

Now create similar arrangements for the following ideas. On line e, add your own arrangement. Then select the one that best fits the given context.

1

IDEA ARRANGEMENTS:

(a) Wealthy people commonly bought the earliest automobiles.

(b) _____

(c) _____

(d) _____

(e) _____

CONTEXT:

_____and were regarded more as toys than as transportation.

2

IDEA ARRANGEMENTS:

(a) _____

(b) Coded messages are rapidly transmitted by weather forecasters.

(c) _____

(d) _____

(e) _____

CONTEXT:

All nations cooperate in preparing accurate weather forecasts. _____
_____eliminates the need to translate from one language to another.

3

IDEA ARRANGEMENTS:

(a) _____

(b) _____

(c) The deliberate biting of people by tarantulas ...

(d) _____

(e) _____

CONTEXT:

The notion that a tarantula's bite will cause a frenzied dance of death is simply not true. _____but do not cause serious illness in their victims.

4

IDEA ARRANGEMENTS:

(a) The SEC rigidly enforces federal securities laws.

(b) _____

(c) _____
(d) _____
(e) _____

CONTEXT:
_____and are never broken without serious conse-
quences. A firm or individual whose practices do not conform to SEC
standards may be subject to criminal prosecution and may be barred
from engaging in the securities business.

MODELED EXERCISE C

IDEA ARRANGEMENTS:
(a) Camels were the answer to the problem.
(b) The answer to the problem was camels.
(c) Camels, the answer to the problem . . .
(d) Camels answered the problem.

Select the arrangement that works best in the following context.

CONTEXT:
During the nineteenth century, transporting military supplies through
the deserts of the American Southwest was very difficult. Some military
people argued that since horses and mules suffered in the hot dry
climate, _____.

*Now create similar arrangements for the following ideas. On line e,
add your own arrangement. Then select the one that best fits the given
context.*

1

IDEA ARRANGEMENTS:
(a) A woman may have been the author of the *Odyssey.*
(b) _____

(c) _____

(d) _____

(e) _____

CONTEXT:

Because the *Odyssey* describes women in a more favorable and realistic light than it does men, some scholars claim that _____
_____.

2

IDEA ARRANGEMENTS:

(a) _____

(b) A supposed protection against disease was garlic.

(c) _____

(d) _____

(e) _____

CONTEXT:

During the Middle Ages, people thought that _____,
could also keep vampires away.

3

IDEA ARRANGEMENTS:

(a) _____

(b) _____

(c) _____

(d) An underground network of old stores attracts visitors.

(e) _____

CONTEXT:

Most tourist attractions are above ground, but in Seattle, Washington,
_____and saloons.

4

IDEA ARRANGEMENTS:

(a) _____

(b) _____

(c) A prison inmate, the inventor of the toothbrush, . . .

(d) _____

(e) _____

CONTEXT:

Not all inventors have been scientists by profession. The inventor of chewing gum was a photographer, while _____.

MODELED EXERCISE D

IDEA ARRANGEMENTS:

(a) After sunset, naturalists search for owls.

(b) Owls are what naturalists search for after sunset.

(c) Owls, for which naturalists search after sunset . . .

(d) Naturalists' searches for owls after sunset . . .

Select the arrangement that works best in the following context.

CONTEXT:

_____, when portable cassette recorders can be used to attract them. As the naturalists play cassettes of an owl's hooting, the owls will often call and fly closer to the recorder.

Now create similar arrangements for the following ideas. On line e, add your own arrangement. Then select the one that best fits the given context.

1

IDEA ARRANGEMENTS:

(a) In the 1920s, young writers thirsted for creative freedom.

(b) _____

(c) _____

(d) _____

(e) _____

CONTEXT:

_____. They found it in Greenwich Village, a section of New York City. Attracted by cheap rents, the young writers were quickly charmed by Greenwich Village's small-town atmosphere. Some, like e.e. cummings, spent the rest of their lives there.

2

IDEA ARRANGEMENTS:
(a) _____
(b) _____
(c) Bargains, for which some people watch nowadays ...
(d) _____
(e) _____

CONTEXT:
_____by reading consumer magazines like *Consumer Reports.* These magazines use laboratory tests to rate the quality of such products as motorized bicycles, radios, pruning tools, and frozen fried chicken.

3

IDEA ARRANGEMENTS:
(a) _____
(b) Treasures are what adventurers hunted for in the nineteenth century.
(c) _____
(d) _____
(e) _____

CONTEXT:
_____were aided by Egyptian guides, who located jewelry and other riches in the tombs of the pharaohs. Despite the loss of many valuable objects, this random treasure hunting led directly to the development of scientific archaeology.

4

IDEA ARRANGEMENTS:
(a) _____
(b) _____
(c) _____
(d) Artists' hopes for new forms of expression today ...
(e) _____

CONTEXT:

_____, could change both the ways artists solve problems and the ways they express emotions. In particular, the introduction of the computer as an artistic tool may have the same dramatic effects that the invention of oil painting and photography had in the past.

MODELED EXERCISE E

IDEA ARRANGEMENTS:
(a) Supposedly, a jealous Italian composer poisoned Mozart.
(b) Supposedly, Mozart was poisoned by a jealous Italian composer.
(c) It is supposed that a jealous Italian composer poisoned Mozart.
(d) The supposition that a jealous Italian composer poisoned Mozart...

Select the arrangement that works best in the following context.

CONTEXT:

_____has been made by several scholars. Unfortunately, it is unlikely that this theory can ever be completely disproved, and so Antonio Salieri will continue to be known as Mozart's murderer rather than as a gifted composer in his own right.

Now create similar arrangements for the following ideas. On line e, add your own arrangement. Then select the one that best fits the given context.

1

IDEA ARRANGEMENTS:
(a) In fact, St. Patrick did not intend to stab the king's foot.
(b) _____
(c) _____
(d) _____
(e) _____

CONTEXT:
During a baptismal rite for an Irish king, St. Patrick's sword slipped. The king said nothing because he thought this maneuver was part of the ceremony. _____with his sword.

2

IDEA ARRANGEMENTS:
(a) _____
(b) Certainly, punched computer cards are known about by most people.
(c) _____
(d) _____
(e) _____

CONTEXT:
In our highly computerized society, _____. What people don't know is that the idea of punched cards was first used over 200 years ago. Jacques Marie Jacquard used the holes in a punched card to "instruct" a loom to weave patterns.

3

IDEA ARRANGEMENTS:
(a) _____
(b) _____
(c) It is surprising that people once believed tomatoes were poisonous.
(d) _____
(e) _____

CONTEXT:
_____—simply because they are related to other plants that are poisonous.

4

IDEA ARRANGEMENTS:
(a) _____
(b) _____
(c) _____
(d) The possibility that Sir Francis Bacon wrote Shakespeare's plays ...
(e) _____

CONTEXT:
Many people have speculated that William Shakespeare's education and background were too common for him to be able to write the extraordinary plays credited to him, but serious historians do not think

OPEN EXERCISE A

The following simple sentences constitute a short essay called "Forecasting Avalanches." Rewrite the sentences as a series of paragraphs. (A gap between lines indicates where a new paragraph should begin.) Remember that you can rearrange some or all of the sentences in the ways you have been shown so far. You can also change punctuation, eliminate unnecessary words, change sentences into phrases, and combine simple sentences in order to form more complex sentences. Keep in mind that there is no single "correct" answer. Compare your finished essay with those of your classmates and be prepared to discuss the choices you have made.

1. A fresh snowfall blankets a mountain range.
2. It looks quiet.
3. It looks peaceful.
4. It looks this way to many people.
5. But not to some scientists.
6. These scientists study the nature of snow.
7. The makeup of snow changes.
8. The change is constant.
9. The makeup responds to weather conditions.
10. It responds to stress.
11. It responds to gravity.
12. These are natural forces.
13. They may fracture the snowcover.
14. This happens in mountain areas.
15. The fracture may unleash masses of snow.
16. The masses take a form.
17. The form is avalanches.
18. Avalanches are violent and destructive.
19. They travel at great speeds.
20. The speeds are up to 200 mph.
21. Avalanches carry rock.
22. They carry earth.
23. They carry other debris.
24. They may bury roads.
25. They may even bury whole towns.

26. There are several ways to forecast avalanches.

27. Scientists have devised them.
28. There is a range of temperatures.
29. The range is within a snowpack.
30. It can be measured.
31. This is one way to forecast an avalanche.
32. There may be a great difference in temperature.
33. The difference may be between two layers of snow.
34. The layers are the top and the bottom.
35. This difference may have a result.
36. The result is an avalanche.
37. There is another way to forecast an aalanche.
38. It is to examine the crystals.
39. The crystals make up the snow.
40. Cup-shaped crystals may be present.
41. This is a sign.
42. It means an avalanche is likely.
43. Avalanches have causes.
44. Many of these are not yet understood.
45. This has an unfortunate result.
46. An avalanche will occur.
47. Just when it will occur cannot be predicted.
48. There is still no way to do this.
49. The way must be reliable.
50. Scientists are studying the problem.
51. They are willing to put up with cold.
52. They are willing to put up with discomfort.
53. They have a reason for this.
54. They know that their work will save lives.

OPEN EXERCISE B

The following simple sentences constitute a short essay called "The Thirty-Eight States of America." Rewrite the sentences as a series of paragraphs. (A gap between lines indicates where a new paragraph should begin.) Remember that you can rearrange some or all of the sentences in the ways you have been shown so far. You can also change punctuation, eliminate unnecessary words, change sentences into phrases, and combine simple sentences in order to form more complex sentences. Keep in mind that there is no single "correct" answer. Compare your finished essay with those of your classmates and be prepared to discuss the choices you have made.

1. G. Etzel Pearcy sees problems.
2. The problems are with the current division of the United States.
3. The United States is divided into 50 states.
4. The states vary widely in population.
5. The states vary widely in area.
6. Pearcy's remedy is a division of the country into 38 states.
7. The states would be new.

8. Original boundary lines were drawn at a certain time.
9. At that time divisions were made along physical boundaries.
10. Rivers or mountain ranges are some of these boundaries.
11. Divisions were made along longitude and latitude lines.
12. Today these state boundaries are a problem.
13. They slice right through major metropolitan areas.
14. New York is an example.
15. The New York metropolitan area is part of three states.

16. Pearcy's system has advantages.
17. State boundaries run through certain areas, where possible.
18. These areas are less populated.
19. Another advantage is that the new states are of similar size.
20. Still another benefit would be tax savings.
21. Consolidating 50 states into 38 would have results.
22. One result would be fewer state governments.
23. Another result would be less duplication of effort.

24. The new states have names.
25. The names were invented by Pearcy.
26. He had help from his students.
27. His students are at California State University, Los Angeles.
28. Each new name reflects an aspect of the state.
29. The aspects may be cultural or physical.
30. The name of a new state in northern New England is Kennebec.
31. The new state comprises Maine, Vermont, most of New Hampshire, and a wedge of New York.
32. Piedmont is another new state.

33. It corresponds primarily to northern Georgia.

34. But is this new map a possibility?
35. Members of the Senate could vote for an amendment.
36. One can hardly imagine them doing this.
37. The amendment would change their constituencies.
38. The amendment would eliminate some Senate seats.
39. There are arguments in favor of such a change.
40. They do not outweigh the difficulties in carrying it out.

OPEN EXERCISE C

The following simple sentences constitute a short essay called "The Hunter's Earliest Friend." Rewrite the sentences as a series of paragraphs. (A gap between lines indicates where a new paragraph should begin.) Remember that you can rearrange some or all of the sentences in the ways you have been shown so far. You can also change punctuation, eliminate unnecessary words, change sentences into phrases, and combine simple sentences in order to form more complex sentences. Keep in mind that there is no single "correct" answer. Compare your finished essay with those of your classmates and be prepared to discuss the choices you have made.

1. Humans have domesticated many animals.
2. Dogs were probably the first.
3. Wild dogs were plentiful in southern Europe.
4. They were plentiful in southern Asia.
5. An association took place there.
6. The association was between dogs and humans.
7. This was their earliest association.
8. Experts believe this.
9. The dogs were in packs.
10. Packs attached themselves to tribes.
11. Hunters made up the tribes.
12. The hunters were nomadic.
13. The packs followed the tribes.
14. They fed on the tribes' leavings.

15.   The dogs' presence was helpful.
16.   It helped a tribe.
17.   It did so in various ways.
18.   Game might be scarce.
19.   Dogs provided a source of meat.
20.   Something else was just as important.
21.   Dogs showed alarm.
22.   They did so when danger approached.
23.   Dogs could be counted on to do so.
24.   Some nights were cold.
25.   A dog might sleep next to its companion.
26.   Its companion was human.
27.   The dog could supply body warmth.
28.   Warmth was vital.

29.   Humans began to use dogs in the hunt.
30.   This happened at some point.
31.   The point was in their early association.
32.   Something made this possible.
33.   It was the dogs' loyalty.
34.   This loyalty was natural.
35.   Wild dogs follow their pack leader.
36.   They obey their pack leader.
37.   This behavior is instinctive.
38.   Tame dogs transfer this devotion.
39.   The transfer is to human masters.

40.   Humans and dogs made a winning combination.
41.   They did so as hunters.
42.   They did so later as herders.
43.   Sheep dogs have a history.
44.   Cow dogs do, too.
45.   This history is ancient.
46.   This history is honorable.
47.   These dogs gave help.
48.   The help was in protecting herds.
49.   The protection was against predators.
50.   Without this help, something might have happened.
51.   Early humans might not have been able to keep livestock.
52.   This might have altered the course of human history.

OPEN EXERCISE D

The following simple sentences constitute a short essay called "Petrification Is Not What It Seems." Rewrite the sentences as a series of paragraphs. (A gap between lines indicates where a new paragraph should begin.) Remember that you can rearrange some or all of the sentences in the ways you have been shown so far. You can also change punctuation, eliminate unnecessary words, change sentences into phrases, and combine simple sentences in order to form more complex sentences. Keep in mind that there is no single "correct" answer. Compare your finished essay with those of your classmates and be prepared to discuss the choices you have made.

1. The Petrified Forest is a national park.
2. It is near Holbrook, Arizona.
3. Its name is somewhat overstated.
4. It misleads many visitors.
5. They expect a forest.
6. They expect to find themselves in it.
7. The expected forest is dense and ancient.
8. Its trees have somehow turned to stone.
9. The reality is different.
10. The Petrified Forest is not an actual forest.
11. It ceased to be more than 180 million years ago.
12. There are some logs.
13. They are huge and petrified.
14. There is some petrified wood.
15. It is in many fragments.
16. The fragments are small.
17. These are from the original trees.
18. They are all that remains.

19. Petrified wood is wood.
20. The wood has turned to stone.
21. This is what people think.
22. It is not so.
23. Living matter cannot become stone.
24. Stone cannot become living matter.
25. The first can happen no more than the second.
26. Wood becomes petrified.

27. This happens by a process.
28. It is a process of substitution.
29. It is not a process of transformation.

30. A piece of wood may be buried.
31. It will start to decompose.
32. Water may seep into the wood.
33. The water may contain dissolved minerals.
34. Decomposing cells leave tiny spaces.
35. The water will fill them.
36. The water may deposit minerals.
37. The minerals can replace the wood cells.
38. They can do this entirely.
39. This happens over millions of years.
40. The original piece of wood vanishes.
41. It served as a "mold."
42. A stone replica is left.
43. It is actual.
44. It is identical to the original.
45. It is so in every detail.

PART TWO:

COMBINING

INTRODUCTION

Part One, you may recall, showed you how you can express any one idea in a variety of ways and how each of these might be useful in an appropriate context. The modeled exercises offered you some practice in arranging simple sentences; the open exercises then gave you a chance to combine these sentences into readable, interesting paragraphs.

So far, however, you have had only your judgment and intuition to rely on in your efforts to combine sentences. While judgment and intuition will remain your most valuable tools, you'll find that learning some commonly used sentence combining techniques can help you save time when you write. These techniques will not only enable you to combine sentences more easily; they will also give you the chance to use different sorts of combinations that you might not have thought of on your own.

In Part Two, then, you'll discover specific methods for putting together some common types of sentences. At the same time, you'll learn to recognize the context clues that tell you which of these methods is the most appropriate in a given situation.

Once again, you'll be working on two types of exercises: modeled and open. The open exercises are very much like the ones you worked with in Part One; they are somewhat longer but not much more difficult. The modeled exercises are also no more difficult than those in Part One, but they do *look* a bit different. In order to prepare you for what's to come, let's take a look at a typical Part Two modeled exercise.

The first thing you'll be shown in the exercise is a short list of simple sentences. It might look like this:

SIMPLE SENTENCES:
A battle inspired "The Star Spangled Banner."
It did not occur in the Revolutionary War.
It occurred in the War of 1812.

Then you'll be shown four different ways that these sentences can be combined into a single sentence (or phrase). These four combinations will be your *model* for the rest of the exercise. The model, in this case, might look like this:

COMBINATIONS:

(a) The battle that inspired "The Star Spangled Banner" did not occur in the Revolutionary War, but in the War of 1812.
(b) A battle inspired "The Star Spangled Banner"; it did not occur in the Revolutionary War, but in the War of 1812.
(c) It was in the War of 1812, not the Revolutionary War, that the battle that inspired "The Star Spangled Banner" occurred.
(d) It was a battle—which occurred in the War of 1812, not the Revolutionary War—that inspired "The Star Spangled Banner."

Just as in the Part One exercises, you'll be asked to decide which of the four combinations works best in a particular context. As usual, remember that there is not necessarily any one "correct" answer. Our sample exercise continues:

Select the combination that works best in the following context.

CONTEXT:
War has been the inspiration for many national anthems. For instance,

_____.

If you try each combination in turn, you'll discover that combination (d) is the one that works best when inserted in the blank. Of the four, only (d) puts its emphasis almost entirely on the word **battle,** and this is most appropriate for a context that is talking specifically about war. As before, however, you'll want to compare your choice with those of your classmates and explain your reasons for choosing as you did.

The exercise continues, as you might expect, with a numbered section that refers back to the model:

Now create similar combinations for the following sets of simple sentences. On line e, add your own combination. Then select the one that best fits the given context.

1

SIMPLE SENTENCES:
One northern European animal is known as a reindeer.
It does not belong to the deer species.
It belongs to the caribou family.

COMBINATIONS:
(a) _____
(b) _____
(c) _____
(d) _____
(e) _____

CONTEXT:
The reindeer looks very much like a deer. But _____.

With your long experience in imitating models, you should have no
trouble coming up with the following solution:

(a) The northern European animal known as a reindeer does not
    belong to the deer species, but to the caribou family.
(b) One northern European animal is known as a reindeer; it does
    not belong to the deer species, but to the caribou family.
(c) It is to the caribou family, not the deer species, that the northern
    European animal known as a reindeer belongs.
(d) It is a northern European animal—which belongs to the caribou
    family, not the deer species—that is known as a reindeer.
(e) [Your choice]

The combination that works best when inserted in the context is (c).

Let's try another section of the same exercise, based on the same
model:

2

SIMPLE SENTENCES:
A virus causes the common cold.
It is not passed primarily through the air.
It is passed primarily through physical contact.

COMBINATIONS:
(a) _____
(b) _____
(c) _____
(d) _____
(e) _____

CONTEXT:
Many people still think that standing outside in cold weather causes colds. But _____.

Once again, you have to refer back to the model in order to work out the right combinations. Your solution should look like this:

(a) The virus that causes the common cold is not passed primarily through the air, but through physical contact.
(b) A virus causes the common cold; it is not passed primarily through the air, but through physical contact.
(c) It is primarily through physical contact, not through the air, that the virus that causes the common cold is passed.
(d) It is a virus—which is passed primarily through physical contact, not through the air—that causes the common cold.
(e) [Your choice]

In this case, the combination that fits best in the context is (b).

The last section of each modeled exercise includes a slightly new twist—a taste of freedom that you weren't given in Part One. You'll be given a list of simple sentences as before, but the list will be incomplete. Before you can combine the sentences according to the model, you'll have to complete the list with your own ideas. As a result, the finished sentence combinations will say what *you* want them to say. Here's how such a section might look, using the same model we've been using all along:

4

Complete the simple sentences by filling in the blanks. Then create a set of combinations as before.

SIMPLE SENTENCES:

A vital ingredient makes good pizza worth eating.

It is not _____.

It is _____.

COMBINATIONS:

(a) _____

(b) _____

(c) _____

(d) _____

(e) _____

This section could be completed in any number of different ways. Simply for demonstration purposes, however, let's say you prefer sauce to cheese. Your completed exercise, in that case, might look like this:

SIMPLE SENTENCES:

A vital ingredient makes good pizza worth eating.

It is not the cheese.

It is the sauce.

COMBINATIONS:

(a) The vital ingredient that makes good pizza worth eating is not the cheese, but the sauce.

(b) A vital ingredient makes good pizza worth eating; it is not the cheese, but the sauce.

(c) It is the sauce, not the cheese, which is the vital ingredient that makes good pizza worth eating.

(d) It is a vital ingredient—which is the sauce, not the cheese—that makes good pizza worth eating.

(e) [Your choice]

Obviously, you won't find any context paragraph in this part of the exercise; nothing we could have written in advance would cover all the possible opinions that you might fill in. Even so, it's a good idea for you to examine the five combinations you've come up with and decide which are the most useful for different situations. You might decide that combination (d), for example, is somewhat awkward and should be avoided altogether.

Now that you're familiar with the sort of exercise you'll be working with, you're ready to go on to the heart of the book—a systematic look at many techniques of sentence combining. Part Two contains four main sections, each of which examines a different type of idea that you may want to express in a piece of writing. Within each section, you'll find a minimum of explanation and a generous number of exercises. The more carefully you do these exercises, the more flexible and interesting your writing will become. You may also find that skillful writing can be challenging, rewarding, and fun.

ASSOCIATION

As you discovered in Part One, the quickest way to combine any two sentences is to link them together with **and.** Take the following set of simple sentences:

> Picasso began to experiment with cubism.
> Braque immediately took a similar turn.
> Their paintings soon could not be told apart.

With the simple addition of **and** (plus a comma, for a more natural rhythm), these sentences become a paragraph:

> Picasso began to experiment with cubism, and Braque immediately took a similar turn. Their paintings soon could not be told apart.

Putting **and** and the comma in a different spot yields a paragraph with a slightly different emphasis:

> Picasso began to experiment with cubism. Braque immediately took a similar turn, and their paintings soon could not be told apart.

And is quite a useful linking word, so long as it is not overused. Other common conjunctions, such as **or** and **but,** can be equally handy for turning separate sentences into a single, continuous thought. By making use of **and, or, but** and a few other words and phrases, we can take independent ideas and put them together in the reader's mind— we can, in other words, associate these ideas for the reader. In this section, **Association,** we'll be looking at a number of techniques for making connections between ideas. You'll find out how best to use common conjunctions, and how to avoid them when the surrounding context would make their use awkward.

Similar Sentences

Among the easiest sentences to combine are groups of sentences that are very similar to each other. Take, for example, the following sets of simple sentences:

An octagon has eight equal sides.
An octagon has eight equal angles.

Harry Houdini produced his own films.
Harry Houdini starred in his own films.

Hitler was a vegetarian.
Gandhi was a vegetarian.

By linking the dissimilar parts of these sentences together, we can turn each pair of sentences into a single statement:

An octagon has eight equal sides and eight equal angles.

Harry Houdini produced and starred in his own films.

Hitler and Gandhi were vegetarians.

You'll notice that each of these combinations follows the same basic formula: whenever two sentences are alike except for one part, the unlike parts can be joined by **and** and the repetition can be left out. Although using **and** is the simplest way of linking these sorts of sentences, it is not by any means the only way. Here, for instance, are some different combinations of the same sentences:

An octagon has eight equal angles as well as eight equal sides.

Harry Houdini produced his own films, in which he also starred.

Both Hitler and Gandhi were vegetarians.

Whether you substitute other words for **and** (such as **as well as, also,** or **in addition to**) or attach other words to it (such as **both** or **even**), you can change the sound and the emphasis of the simple sentences you combine. (**Both Hitler and Gandhi were vegetarians,** for example, draws more attention to the dissimilarity of the two men than does the simple **Hitler and Gandhi were vegetarians.**) As you do the exercises in this section, you'll become more familiar with the ways **and** and its substitutes can be used to produce a variety of effects.

Remember: Do all your work on a separate sheet of paper. Don't write in the book.

MODELED EXERCISE A

SIMPLE SENTENCES:
A girl pitcher once struck out Babe Ruth.
A girl pitcher once struck out Lou Gehrig.

COMBINATIONS:
(a) A girl pitcher once struck out both Babe Ruth and Lou Gehrig.
(b) Both Babe Ruth and Lou Gehrig were once struck out by a girl pitcher.
(c) A girl pitcher who once struck out both Babe Ruth and Lou Gehrig . . .
(d) Babe Ruth was once struck out by a girl pitcher who also struck out Lou Gehrig.

Select the combination that works best in the following context.

CONTEXT:
_____who was only 17 years old. Both men later said that although the strikeouts took place during an exhibition game, they were the real thing and not simply publicity stunts.

Now create similar combinations for the following sets of simple sentences. On line e, add your own combination. Then select the one that best fits the given context.

1

SIMPLE SENTENCES:
Dr. Frederick Cook explored the Arctic.
Dr. Frederick Cook explored the Antarctic.

COMBINATIONS:
(a) _____
(b) _____
(c) _____
(d) _____
(e) _____

CONTEXT:
Although his claim to the discovery of the North Pole is probably fraudulent, nineteenth century explorer _____.

2

SIMPLE SENTENCES:
A disastrous earthquake leveled Tokyo.
A disastrous earthquake leveled Yokohama.

COMBINATIONS:
(a) _____
(b) _____
(c) _____
(d) _____
(e) _____

CONTEXT:
_____killed 99,000 and left 1,500,000 homeless.

3

SIMPLE SENTENCES:
Thomas Alva Edison invented the electric light bulb.
Thomas Alva Edison invented the phonograph.

COMBINATIONS:
(a) _____
(b) _____

(c) _____
(d) _____
(e) _____

CONTEXT:

_____, the motion picture camera and projector, and the Wall Street stock ticker.

4

Complete the simple sentences by filling in the blanks. Then create a set of combinations as before.

SIMPLE SENTENCES:

Shoppers making a major purchase should compare _____ _____.

Shoppers making a major purchase should compare _____ _____.

COMBINATIONS:

(a) _____
(b) _____
(c) _____
(d) _____
(e) _____

OPEN EXERCISE A

The following simple sentences constitute a short essay called "What Is Primitive Art?" Rewrite the sentences in essay form. (A gap between lines indicates that you should start a new paragraph.) You will notice that sentences 1–2 and 62–63 are of the type you have worked with in the previous exercise. Compare your finished essay with those of your classmates and be prepared to discuss the choices you have made.

1. Seeing primitive art for the first time can astonish students.
2. Seeing primitive art for the first time can astonish other museum-goers.

3. They are accustomed to European art.
4. Primitive art collections contain treasures.
5. The treasures include wooden masks.
6. The treasures include gold drinking cups.
7. The treasures include stone ornaments.
8. The treasures include shields.
9. The shields are decorated with shells.
10. Examining these treasures can be exciting.
11. There is a reason for this excitement.
12. Examining these treasures exposes people to lands and cultures.
13. The lands and cultures were previously unknown or misunderstood.
14. Primitive art comes from Africa.
15. Primitive art comes from Oceania.
16. Primitive art comes from the Americas.
17. It is the work of ancient cultures.
18. They rely on tools rather than machines.
19. Primitive art often seems puzzling at first.
20. Its beauty has an effect on people.
21. The effect is powerful.
22. The effect is almost magical.

23. Primitive people used earspools to adorn themselves.
24. Primitive people used pendants to adorn themselves.
25. Primitive people used breastplates to adorn themselves.
26. Primitive people used nose ornaments to adorn themselves.
27. This adornment revealed a love of beauty.
28. This adornment revealed a love of self expression.
29. Some of the art objects had practical uses.
30. Examples of these objects are stone clubs and ceramic jars.
31. They are not necessarily simple.
32. They are not necessarily crude.
33. Beautifully decorated canoes were obviously useful.
34. Debating stools were obviously useful.
35. Fly swatters were obviously useful.
36. Images of gods were also useful.
37. So were grave markers.
38. So were charms.
39. These objects were weapons.
40. They were used to free people.

41. They freed people from the rule of spirits.
42. They were used to help hunters.
43. They were used to control the weather.
44. Rattles were used in religious observances.
45. Masks were used in religious observances.
46. Initiations are examples of these observances.
47. Harvest ceremonies are examples of these observances.
48. Some images were symbols of royal power.
49. Other images equipped graves for life after death.

50. Primitive art works were once collected as curiosities.
51. Primitive art works were once sold as curiosities.
52. Primitive art works were studied seriously only after 1850.
53. Some young artists began collecting primitive art.
54. They began their collections in the early 1900s.
55. The artists were to become the leaders of a movement.
56. It was the modern art movement.
57. The magical power of primitive art appealed to artists.
58. The freedom of primitive art appealed to artists.
59. Two of these artists were Pablo Picasso and Henri Matisse.
60. This appeal had a result.
61. The result was that primitive art had an influence.
62. It influenced modern painting.
63. It influenced modern sculpture.
64. More recently, black artists have shown an awareness.
65. This awareness is of their heritage.
66. Their heritage is African.
67. Art museums have begun collections.
68. The collections are of primitive art.
69. Today appreciation of primitive art is increasing.
70. New discoveries are constantly being made.

MODELED EXERCISE B

SIMPLE SENTENCES:
The horseshoe crab is a prehistoric animal.
It is alive today.
The crocodile is a prehistoric animal.
It also is alive today.

COMBINATIONS:

(a) Both the horseshoe crab and the crocodile are prehistoric animals that are alive today.
(b) Like the horseshoe crab, the crocodile is a prehistoric animal that is alive today.
(c) Prehistoric animals still alive today include the horseshoe crab and the crocodile.
(d) The horseshoe crab and the crocodile, both prehistoric animals that are alive today, . . .

Select the combination that works best in the following context.

CONTEXT:
Although we tend to think prehistoric animals are extinct, two common

_____.

Now create similar combinations for the following sets of simple sentences. On line e, add your own combination. Then select the one that best fits the given context.

1

SIMPLE SENTENCES:
George Bernard Shaw was a creative person.
He continued to work beyond the age of 90.
Pablo Picasso was a creative person.
He also continued to work beyond the age of 90.

COMBINATIONS:

(a) _____
(b) _____
(c) _____
(d) _____
(e) _____

CONTEXT:
For some, creative genius seems to go hand in hand with longevity.

_____.

2

SIMPLE SENTENCES:
George Washington is a president.
His face appears on U.S. currency.
Woodrow Wilson is a president.
His face also appears on U.S. currency.

COMBINATIONS:

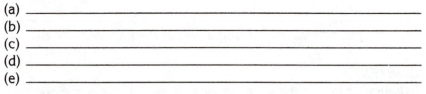

(a) _____
(b) _____
(c) _____
(d) _____
(e) _____

CONTEXT:
_____. But few people will ever see his picture in their wallets, since it appears on the $100,000 bill.

3

SIMPLE SENTENCES:
Esperanto is an artificial language.
Esperanto is based on Indo-European root words.
Ido is an artificial language.
Ido is also based on Indo-European root words.

COMBINATIONS:

(a) _____
(b) _____
(c) _____
(d) _____
(e) _____

CONTEXT:
_____, were invented with the hope of creating a universal language that would improve international communication.

4

Complete the simple sentences by filling in the blanks. Then create a set of combinations as before.

SIMPLE SENTENCES:

_____is a good writer.

[S]he usually writes _____.

_____is a good writer.

[S]he also usually writes _____.

COMBINATIONS:

(a) _____

(b) _____

(c) _____

(d) _____

(e) _____

OPEN EXERCISE B

The following simple sentences constitute a short essay called "Inexpensive Decorating." Rewrite the sentences in essay form. (A gap between lines indicates that you should start a new paragraph.) You will notice that sentences 6–7, 18–19, 23–24, 38–39, and 41–42 are of the type you have worked with in the previous exercise. Compare your finished essay with those of your classmates and be prepared to discuss the choices you have made.

1. People come home at the end of the day.
2. It is nice to come home to an attractive apartment.
3. It is nice to come home to an attractive house.
4. But creating that environment is difficult for some people.
5. These people are on shoestring budgets.
6. Students are among these people.
7. Entry-level employees are among these people.

8. Two inexpensive items can make the job easier.
9. The first is paint.
10. There is nothing like a coat of paint.
11. Nothing can improve a drab room as quickly and inexpensively.
12. A light color will make a room seem larger.
13. A dark color will make a room seem smaller.
14. A dark color will make a room seem more intimate.

15. Talk to your landlord.
16. Do this before you begin to paint the walls.
17. The landlord may want to okay the paint color.
18. Orange is a color.
19. Black is a color.
20. You may like them.
21. They may not please the next tenant.
22. Paint can also do a lot for old furniture.
23. A garage sale dresser is not to be scorned.
24. The bed from your old bedroom is not to be scorned.
25. They may be painted to match each other.
26. Then they will probably look fine.

27. Paint can be a big help.
28. This is true of inexpensive fabric also.
29. Sheets come in tailored patterns.
30. Sheets come in floral patterns.
31. They can be used to make a tablecloth.
32. They can be used to make a quick slipcover.
33. The slipcover can be used for an upholstered chair.
34. Sheets can be used to make curtains.
35. A sheet can even be stapled on the wall.
36. It can be a substitute for wallpaper.
37. The substitute is good-looking.

38. Paint can be used well.
39. Fabric can be used well.
40. Using them well will have a result.
41. Paint will be an economical answer to decorating problems.
42. Fabric will be an economical answer to decorating problems.

MODELED EXERCISE C

SIMPLE SENTENCES:
Hunters sought out great auks.
Hunters killed great auks.

COMBINATIONS:
(a) Hunters sought out and killed great auks.
(b) Hunters killed the great auks that they sought out.

(c) Great auks were sought out and killed by hunters.
(d) Hunters not only sought out great auks; they killed them.

Select the combination that works best in the following context.

CONTEXT:
Since their bodies could provide valuable oil, _____. In
fact, the penguin-like birds were eventually hunted to extinction. The
last living specimen was seen on October 3, 1844.

*Now create similar combinations for the following sets of simple sen-
tences. On line e, add your own combination. Then select the one
that best fits the given context.*

1

SIMPLE SENTENCES:
Nikola Tesla invented a tiny oscillator.
Nikola Tesla smashed the tiny oscillator.

COMBINATIONS:
(a) _____
(b) _____
(c) _____
(d) _____
(e) _____

CONTEXT:
Because he could not stop the vibrations coming from his new machine, _____. The scientist knew of no other way to stop
the vibrations.

2

SIMPLE SENTENCES:
Vincent Van Gogh threatened his friend.
Vincent Van Gogh attacked his friend.

COMBINATIONS:
(a) _____
(b) _____

(c) _____
(d) _____
(e) _____

CONTEXT:

_____, the painter Paul Gauguin. Then he cut off a piece of his own ear to punish himself. This incident was only the first of Van Gogh's many bouts of insanity.

3

SIMPLE SENTENCES:
Leaves capture energy from sunlight.
Leaves use energy from sunlight.

COMBINATIONS:
(a) _____
(b) _____
(c) _____
(d) _____
(e) _____

CONTEXT:

_____to make food. Plants are the only living creatures that can convert solar energy into chemical energy.

4

Complete the simple sentences by filling in the blanks. Then create a set of combinations as before.

SIMPLE SENTENCES:
Governments _____people.
Governments _____people.

COMBINATIONS:
(a) _____
(b) _____

(c) _____
(d) _____
(e) _____

OPEN EXERCISE C

The following simple sentences constitute a short essay called "Enlightening Facts About Lightning." Rewrite the sentences in essay form. (A gap between lines indicates that you should start a new paragraph.) You will notice that sentences 3–4 and 45–46 are of the type you have worked with in the previous exercise. Compare your finished essay with those of your classmates and be prepared to discuss the choices you have made.

1. Lightning strikes fear in the hearts of many people.
2. Perhaps this is for a good reason.
3. Lightning wounds people.
4. Lightning kills people.
5. It does these things to more people combined than any other natural disaster.
6. This is true in the United States.
7. Lightning also destroys property.
8. It destroys millions of dollars' worth.
9. This does not include the losses from forest fires.
10. Yet, there are positive facts about lightning.
11. Some of them may make lightning less intimidating.

12. You see a streak of light in the sky.
13. You think it is moving down.
14. Actually it is moving up.
15. The light starts at the first point of contact.
16. It hurtles up to the cloud.
17. The streak of light appears to be moving down.
18. The downward movement is an optical illusion.
19. This is a fact.
20. The illusion is created by the light's movement.
21. The movement is faster than your eye can follow.

22. Lightning usually makes contact with the highest point in an area.
23. Its current follows the best conducting path offered.
24. This is why a lightning rod is successful.
25. Its success is in dissipating the electrical charge.
26. However, no path may be offered.
27. Then lightning makes a path of its own.
28. Lightning does this brutally.
29. Lightning may strike you.
30. Your clothes may be wet.
31. These conditions would have a result.
32. The result is that the current would pass through your wet clothes.
33. You might survive such an experience.
34. Lightning may strike a tree.
35. The bark of the tree may be dry.
36. These conditions would have a result.
37. The result is that the current would pass through the wet sap in the bark.
38. The sap would quickly be heated to steam.
39. The steam would expand abruptly.
40. This would cause the tree to explode.

41. Lightning is vital to life.
42. It enables plant life to exist.
43. Perhaps this is the most important fact about lightning.
44. Plants need nitrogen to make proteins.
45. Without these proteins, they could not live.
46. Without these proteins, they could not grow.
47. Nitrogen is in the atmosphere.
48. Nitrogen must undergo a series of chemical reactions.
49. Before that, plants cannot use it.
50. Lightning touches off this series of reactions.
51. Hence, lightning is necessary.
52. It is equally awesome.
53. You may encounter an electrical storm.
54. The next time this happens, do three things.
55. Find a safe shelter.
56. Think about the preceding positive facts.
57. Enjoy the spectacle.

MODELED EXERCISE D

SIMPLE SENTENCES:
The Model T freed farmers from isolation.
Then it did something else.
It helped them with chores.

COMBINATIONS:
(a) The Model T freed farmers from isolation and helped them with chores.
(b) The Model T helped farmers with chores after freeing them from isolation.
(c) The Model T not only freed farmers from isolation; it helped them with chores as well.
(d) By freeing farmers from isolation and then helping them with chores, the Model T...

Select the combination that works best in the following context.

CONTEXT:
_____, such as taking grain to local elevators. Autos were even used to carry water to livestock and to rope and brand calves.

Now create similar combinations for the following sets of simple sentences. On line e, add your own combination. Then select the one that best fits the given context.

1

SIMPLE SENTENCES:
The Kwakiutl Indians accumulated wealth.
Then they did something else.
They gave it away.

COMBINATIONS:
(a) _____
(b) _____

(c) _____

(d) _____

(e) _____

CONTEXT:

_____earned status in their tribe. Those who gave away the greatest amount of riches became the most powerful and re-spected members of the community.

2

SIMPLE SENTENCES:

The barracuda engulfs small fish.

Then it does something else.

It allows them to escape.

COMBINATIONS:

(a) _____

(b) _____

(d) _____

(d) _____

(e) _____

CONTEXT:

_____is able to get rid of parasites. The small fish pick them off its teeth and flee quickly with their food.

3

SIMPLE SENTENCES:

Ultrasound devices create pictures of interior organs.

Then they do something else.

They detect flaws in them.

COMBINATIONS:

(a) _____

(b) _____

(c) _____

(d) _____

(e) _____

CONTEXT:

_____with high-frequency sound waves.

4

Insert your own simple sentence in the blank. Then create a set of combinations as before.

SIMPLE SENTENCES:
Young people sometimes make plans.
Then they do something else.

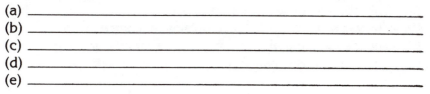

COMBINATIONS:
(a) _____
(b) _____
(c) _____
(d) _____
(e) _____

OPEN EXERCISE D

The following simple sentences constitute a short essay called "The Extravagant Society." Sentences 51 through 60 are missing; you will have to supply these yourself. (The general topic of the sentences you write should be Americans' wastefulness of their natural resources. Feel free to add more or fewer than the specified number of sentences if you think that doing so will improve the essay.)

Rewrite the sentences in essay form. (A gap between lines indicates that you should start a new paragraph.) You will notice that sentences 40–41 and 42–45 are of the type you have worked with in the previous section. Some of the sentences you supply should be of this type as well.

Compare your finished essay with those of your classmates and be prepared to discuss the choices you have made.

1. Americans are often called wasteful.
2. We are called the most wasteful people on earth.
3. Our trash cans overflow.
4. They overflow with uneaten food.

5.   They overflow with unnecessary packaging.
6.   Our industries squander raw materials.
7.   Our industries squander manpower.
8.   The squandering happens through poor planning.
9.   The squandering happens through poor management.

10.   There are reasons for our wastefulness.
11.   They can be found in our history.
12.   The earliest immigrants came from Europe.
13.   They found an abundance of land.
14.   They found an abundance of natural resources.
15.   This abundance was breathtaking.
16.   The vastness of the American plains reinforced an idea.
17.   The idea was that the nation would never lack anything.
18.   The nation was expanding.

19.   Americans experienced the Great Depression.
20.   Then their attitudes toward wastefulness changed.
21.   The Great Depression was in the 1930s.
22.   Prudence was essential during that time.
23.   Thrift was essential during that time.
24.   Then came World War II.
25.   Americans learned a different lesson at that time.
26.   Some raw materials were unavailable.
27.   Technology came to the rescue.
28.   Rubber could no longer be imported.
29.   It had been imported from southeast Asia.
30.   Southeast Asia was held by the Japanese.
31.   American scientists invented synthetic rubber.
32.   This kind of success gave many Americans an idea.
33.   The idea was unfortunate.
34.   The idea was that technology could solve a problem.
35.   The problem was that of diminishing resources.

36.   America returned to its wasteful ways.
37.   It did this after the war.
38.   Industry introduced "planned obsolescence."
39.   This was the idea that we could use a product for a few years.
40.   Then we could throw it away.
41.   Then we could buy a newer model.

42. Americans drove cars.
43. The cars were big.
44. Americans used gas.
45. They used it freely.
46. There was an energy crisis in the seventies.
47. It took the energy crisis to bring home a need.
48. The need was to conserve.
49. Americans have an increasing awareness of scarce resources.
50. Even so, Americans continue to be wasteful.
51. _____
52. _____
53. _____
54. _____
55. _____
56. _____
57. _____
58. _____
59. _____
60. _____
61. Recycling programs could make a change.
62. New laws could make a change.
63. New attitudes and habits could make a change.
64. They could make America a less extravagant place.
65. This could happen in the future.

Dissimilar Sentences

In the exercises you've done so far in this section, you've been combining sentences that are similar to each other in one way or another. Often, however, you'll find that you want to combine sentences that are quite *dis*similar, simply to associate them in the reader's mind. Our reliable linking word **and** can do this under some circumstances, but in many cases the use of **and** will lead to awkwardness or confusion. Take, for example, the following groups of simple sentences:

America's steel imports have grown tremendously.
Domestic steel manufacturers are suffering.

European critics admired Poe's poetry.
American critics found it vague and mechanical.

Old legal documents were written by hand.
The typewriter is a fairly recent invention.

When we use the word **and** to link each pair of sentences (along with a comma, for proper rhythm), we get the following combinations:

America's steel imports have grown tremendously, and domestic steel manufacturers are suffering.

European critics admired Poe's poetry, and American critics found it vague and mechanical.

Old legal documents were written by hand, and the typewriter is a fairly recent invention.

As you can see, joining sentences with **and** can have quite unpredictable results. The first combination seems fine; the second sounds a little awkward; and the third seems to make no sense at all. Fortunately, the English language offers us other words besides **and** that can be used to link sentences together; the most common of these are **but, or,** and **except. But** is a particularly flexible word—it combines sentences as simply as **and** does, but it also points out the *differences* between what two sentences are saying:

America's steel imports have grown tremendously, but domestic steel manufacturers are suffering.

European critics admired Poe's poetry, but American critics found it vague and mechanical.

You'll notice, however, that **but** does not work with every set of dissimilar sentences. We can't, for instance, say:

Old legal documents were written by hand, but the typewriter is a fairly recent invention.

As before, the sentence makes no sense—and it would still make no sense if we replaced **but** with **or** or **except.** (You can try that on your own.) In situations like this one, you can always fall back on a simple and elegant connecting device—the semicolon. When you combine two sentences with a semicolon, you are simply indicating that these sentences are connected in some way—but in *what* way is up to the reader to decide. It is perfectly proper, therefore, to write:

Old legal documents were written by hand; the typewriter is a fairly recent invention.

For that matter, you can also write:

America's steel imports have grown tremendously; domestic steel manufacturers are suffering.

European critics admired Poe's poetry; American critics found it vague and mechanical.

The exercises that make up the remainder of this section will give you an opportunity to use **and, but,** and the semicolon in a variety of situations. You'll also be using some other connecting words and phrases, such as **or** and **except,** that express contrast in ways that **but** does not. Remember that these exercises do not cover all the possible ways in which dissimilar sentences can be linked; they are simply suggestions that you, with a bit of imagination, can use to make your writing more flexible.

MODELED EXERCISE A

SIMPLE SENTENCES:
A volcano erupted near Java.
Temperatures dropped in North America.
This occurred soon afterward.

COMBINATIONS:
(a) A volcano erupted near Java, and temperatures dropped in North America soon afterward.
(b) A volcano erupted near Java; soon afterward, temperatures dropped in North America.

(c) Temperatures dropped in North America soon after a volcano erupted near Java.

(d) A drop in temperatures in North America occurred soon after a volcano erupted near Java.

Select the combination that works best in the following context.

CONTEXT:
On April 5, 1815, _____and in western Europe. The eruption continued to affect the world's weather for more than a year after it occurred. Connecticut, for example, was hit by a blizzard on June 16, 1816.

Now create similar combinations for the following sets of simple sentences. On line e, add your own combination. Then select the one that best fits the given context.

1

SIMPLE SENTENCES:
Mill owners began to employ Irish immigrants.
The mills' work force changed drastically.
This occurred within a few years.

COMBINATIONS:
(a) _____
(b) _____
(c) _____
(d) _____
(e) _____

CONTEXT:
The Irish potato famine of the 1840s proved to be a boon for New England's textile mills. A huge increase in production and _____

_____.

2

SIMPLE SENTENCES:
The hydrogen cloud collided with the earth.
There were disturbances in the earth's magnetic field.
This happened almost immediately afterward.

COMBINATIONS:

(a) _____

(b) _____

(c) _____

(d) _____

(e) _____

CONTEXT:

On November 12, 1960, astronomers detected an explosion on the surface of the sun. The explosion released a tremendous cloud of hydrogen gas. Six hours passed before _____. Compass needles wavered, and sheets of red light in the northern night sky lasted for more than a week.

3

SIMPLE SENTENCES:

Taylor's inauguration was put off for a day.
David Atchison became our country's only one-day President.
This occurred as a result.

COMBINATIONS:

(a) _____

(b) _____

(c) _____

(d) _____

(e) _____

CONTEXT:

President James Polk's term expired on Saturday, March 3, but President-elect Zachary Taylor refused to be sworn into office on a Sunday. _____of the postponement. Atchison, the president pro tempore of the Senate, accomplished nothing of consequence during his brief tenure as Chief Executive.

4

Complete the simple sentences by filling in the blanks. Then create a set of combinations as before.

SIMPLE SENTENCES:

_____was invented.

_____lost its usefulness.

This occurred _____.

COMBINATIONS:

(a) _____

(b) _____

(c) _____

(d) _____

(e) _____

OPEN EXERCISE A

The following simple sentences constitute a short essay called "Old Ironsides." Rewrite the sentences in essay form. (A gap between lines indicates that you should start a new paragraph.) You will notice that sentences 33 through 36 are of the type you have worked with in the previous exercise. Compare your finished essay with those of your classmates and be prepared to discuss the choices you have made.

1. There are some famous American fighting ships.
2. One of the most famous was a frigate.
3. It was made from cedar and oak.
4. It was called "Old Ironsides."
5. It was built in Boston in 1797.
6. It was officially christened the *Constitution*.
7. It became known as "Old Ironsides."
8. At first this was because of how the ship was built.
9. It was built differently from other ships.
10. Its oak planks were bent into place.
11. This was done without the use of steam.
12. The use of steam was customary.
13. It made construction easier.
14. It also weakened the wood.
15. Later, the nickname stuck.
16. This happened in battle.
17. A solid shot hit the ship.
18. It glanced harmlessly from the ship's side.

19. A gunner saw this happen.
20. He exclaimed, "Her sides must be made of iron!"

21. The *Constitution* took part in the War of 1812.
22. It achieved its greatest glory in this war.
23. Its fleetness and strength were tested.
24. The test was against British ships.
25. They were the greatest in the British navy.
26. "Old Ironsides" triumphed over these ships.
27. They are now forgotten.
28. One such ship was the *Guerrière*.
29. Another was the *Java*.
30. Another was the *Cyane*.
31. Still another was the *Levant*.

32. Steamships were invented and adopted.
33. This made certain naval boats obsolete.
34. These obsolete boats were those propelled by sails.
35. The navy ordered that the *Constitution* be broken up.
36. This was inevitable.
37. The order was given in 1830.
38. The great ship was saved by a poem.
39. It had three stanzas.
40. It was published in the *Boston Daily Advertiser*.
41. It was written by Oliver Wendell Holmes.
42. At that time he was unknown.
43. The poem was called "Old Ironsides."
44. It protested the proposed breaking up of the *Constitution*.
45. It motivated people to prevent the ship's destruction.
46. Later, the ship was reconstructed.
47. Its reconstruction began in 1925.
48. It was made possible by an act of Congress.
49. It was funded by donations.
50. These were made largely by schoolchildren.
51. "Old Ironsides" has been put to sea again.
52. This time it is a naval museum.
53. "Old Ironsides" is currently berthed in Boston.
54. It is a permanent unit of the United States Navy.
55. This is now official.

MODELED EXERCISE B

SIMPLE SENTENCES:
London's first department stores seemed pleasant.
They were disagreeable places to work.

COMBINATIONS:
(a) London's first department stores seemed pleasant, but they were disagreeable places to work.
(b) Although they were disagreeable places to work, London's first department stores seemed pleasant.
(c) London's first department stores seemed pleasant even though they were disagreeable places to work.
(d) It is surprising that London's first department stores were disagreeable places to work, since they seemed pleasant.

Select the combination that works best in the following context.

CONTEXT:
_____. After fifteen hours of work a day, shop assistants were required to eat and sleep in quarters above the stores, visiting their families only on weekends.

Now create similar combinations for the following sets of simple sentences. On line e, add your own combination. Then select the one that best fits the given context.

1

SIMPLE SENTENCES:
Catfish are usually considered harmless.
The electric catfish can attack with 450-volt shocks.

COMBINATIONS:
(a) _____
(b) _____
(c) _____
(d) _____
(e) _____

CONTEXT:
_____—and even though such a shock can stun a person or a large animal.

2

SIMPLE SENTENCES:
Chocolate may appear to cause acne.
Hormones and hereditary factors are the actual causes.

COMBINATIONS:
(a) _____
(b) _____
(c) _____
(d) _____
(e) _____

CONTEXT:
_____because it is popular among teenagers, many of whom have acne problems.

3

SIMPLE SENTENCES:
The fossils were thought to be dragon bones.
They proved to be dinosaur bones.

COMBINATIONS:
(a) _____
(b) _____
(c) _____
(d) _____
(e) _____

CONTEXT:
The remains of a huge, lizard-like skeleton were found in the seventeenth century. _____. Until the nineteenth century, scientists had no idea that dinosaurs had ever existed.

4

Insert your own simple sentence in the blank. Then create a set of combinations as before.

SIMPLE SENTENCES:
Succeeding in college sometimes looks easy to outsiders.

COMBINATIONS:
(a) _____
(b) _____
(c) _____
(d) _____
(e) _____

OPEN EXERCISE B

The following simple sentences constitute a short essay called "Thomas Jefferson's Monticello." Rewrite the sentences in essay form. (A gap between lines indicates that you should start a new paragraph.) You will notice that sentences 17–18, 28–29, and 33–34 are of the type you have worked with in the previous exercise. Compare your finished essay with those of your classmates and be prepared to discuss the choices you have made.

1. Monticello was Thomas Jefferson's home.
2. Monticello is near Charlottesville, Virginia.
3. Monticello clearly reveals a personality.
4. The personality is that of its owner.
5. Monticello reflects Jefferson's elegance.
6. Monticello reflects Jefferson's imagination.
7. Monticello reflects Jefferson's originality.
8. Jefferson borrowed ideas from the ancient Greeks.
9. Jefferson borrowed ideas from the ancient Romans.
10. He borrowed these ideas for his own home.
11. He was the first American to do so.
12. The imprint of Monticello is on the nickel.
13. The imprint gives some idea of his success.

14. Jefferson was a self-taught architect.
15. Jefferson supervised every detail of the building of Monticello.

16. Jefferson supervised every detail of the furnishing of Monticello.
17. Outbuildings were usually visible around the houses of the time.
18. Jefferson devised a way to hide his outbuildings.
19. He hid them beneath long terraces.
20. The terraces extended from the house.
21. The inside of the house revealed Jefferson's love of gadgets.
22. It revealed Jefferson's love of innovations.
23. Inside the house he had skylights.
24. Inside the house he had a revolving serving door.
25. Inside the house he had an alcove bed.
26. The bed was open on both sides.
27. Inside the house he had a seven-day calendar clock.
28. The weathervane was outside the house.
29. The weathervane could be read from inside.
30. Jefferson also owned a machine.
31. The machine made extra copies of his letters.
32. It made the copies as he wrote the letters.

33. Monticello is now open to the public.
34. The work of restoring it continues.
35. Archaeologists are digging up the foundations of buildings.
36. The buildings were used for weaving.
37. The buildings were used for smoking meat.
38. The buildings were used for nailmaking.
39. Analysis of the soil helps to determine the layout of Jefferson's gardens.
40. Analysis of the soil helps to determine the layout of Jefferson's orchards.
41. Darker soil can show where a fencepost rotted.
42. This is an example.
43. Infrared photographs are taken from the air.
44. The photographs reveal different kinds of soils.
45. The soils provide hints about land use.
46. The land use was in Jefferson's day.

47. Today, Monticello is a national historic landmark.
48. It is a vivid reminder of Thomas Jefferson.
49. Thomas Jefferson was one of the most versatile men in American history.

MODELED EXERCISE C

SIMPLE SENTENCES:
Beethoven had been growing more deaf every year.
He could no longer converse with his friends.
There was an exception.
He could converse with them through writing.

COMBINATIONS:
(a) Beethoven, who had been growing more deaf every year, could no longer converse with his friends except through writing.
(b) Beethoven had been growing more deaf every year; he could no longer converse with his friends except through writing.
(c) It was only through writing that Beethoven, who had been growing more deaf every year, could still converse with his friends.
(d) Except through writing, Beethoven could no longer converse with his friends; he had been growing more deaf every year.

Select the combination that works best in the following context.

CONTEXT:
When did Beethoven's deafness become total? We know that after 1818, ——————————.

Now create similar combinations for the following sets of simple sentences. On line e, add your own combination. Then select the one that best fits the given context.

1

SIMPLE SENTENCES:
The northern lights were a common sight in northern Europe.
They were not seen in southern Europe.
There were exceptions.
They were seen in southern Europe on rare occasions.

COMBINATIONS:
(a) ——————————————————————————
(b) ——————————————————————————

(c) _____
(d) _____
(e) _____

CONTEXT:

Throughout medieval times, people in northern Europe watched the northern lights without alarm. But _____. As a consequence, southern Europeans feared them as evil omens.

2

SIMPLE SENTENCES:

Edison had failed miserably.
He received no further education.
There was an exception.
He was educated by his mother at home.

COMBINATIONS:

(a) _____
(b) _____
(c) _____
(d) _____
(e) _____

CONTEXT:

As a child, Thomas Edison was considered backward. In his first term at school _____.

3

SIMPLE SENTENCES:

The tropical treefrog sleeps by day.
It does not take on bright colors.
There is an exception.
It takes on bright colors at night.

COMBINATIONS:

(a) _____
(b) _____

(c) _____
(d) _____
(e) _____

CONTEXT:
In order to protect itself from predators, _____. In this regard it differs from other frogs, whose colors tend to fade in darkness.

4

Complete the simple sentences by filling in the blanks. Then create a set of combinations as before.

SIMPLE SENTENCES:
Children are protected by child labor laws.
They cannot _____.
There is an exception.
They can _____.

COMBINATIONS:
(a) _____
(b) _____
(c) _____
(d) _____
(e) _____

OPEN EXERCISE C

The following simple sentences constitute a short essay called "The Deadly Pitcher." Rewrite the sentences in essay form. (A gap between lines indicates that you should start a new paragraph.) You will notice that sentences 13–16 and 19–22 are of the type you have worked with in the previous exercise. Compare your finished essay with those of your classmates and be prepared to discuss the choices you have made.

1. The animal kingdom depends on plants for its food.
2. Some animals eat plants directly.

3. Sheep do so.
4. Others eat plants indirectly.
5. Wolves do so.
6. Wolves eat the sheep.
7. The sheep ate the plants.
8. All animal food can be traced back to plants.
9. Plants are more self-sufficient.
10. They take their nourishment from the soil.
11. They don't need to raid the animal kingdom for food.
12. Do they?

13. Plants live in soil.
14. They don't feed on anything else.
15. There are exceptions.
16. In rare cases they feed on animals as well.
17. One plant feeds both ways.
18. It is the pitcher plant.
19. The soil nourishes this plant.
20. It supplies all needed nutrients.
21. There are exceptions.
22. It does not supply certain needed minerals.
23. The soil lacks these minerals.
24. The plant must get them.
25. It must do so elsewhere.
26. It has evolved a method to do this.
27. It is a method of trapping and eating meat.
28. This method is fascinating.

29. Its leaves give the plant its name.
30. They are pitcher-shaped.
31. They hold water.
32. Nectar attracts insects.
33. It is sweet-smelling.
34. It is on the rim of each pitcher.
35. Wax is just inside the rim.
36. An insect may get a foothold on the wax.
37. This happens sometimes.
38. The wax crumbles.
39. It drops the victim into the pitcher.
40. The victim drowns in the pitcher.

41. All pitcher plants trap insects.
42. One large type can trap other things as well.
43. It can trap mice and birds.
44. The birds are small ones.
45. The pitcher plant digests whatever it catches.
46. The digestion happens right in the pitcher.
47. The plant absorbs what it digests.
48. It absorbs this into itself.

MODELED EXERCISE D

SIMPLE SENTENCES:
The law divides property into two types.
One type is public property.
The other type is private property.

COMBINATIONS:
(a) The law classifies property as either public or private.
(b) According to the law, property is either public or private.
(c) Some property is public, according to the law; the rest is private.
(d) The law divides property into two types: public and private.

Select the combination that works best in the following context.

CONTEXT:
_____. Even if this private property is used for public purposes, it remains "private" in the legal sense so long as it is owned by a person or association.

Now create similar combinations for the following sets of simple sentences. On line e, add your own combination. Then select the one that best fits the given context.

1

SIMPLE SENTENCES:
Cat associations place cats into two categories.
One category is long-haired.
The other category is short-haired.

COMBINATIONS:

(a) _____

(b) _____

(c) _____

(d) _____

(e) _____

CONTEXT:

In the United States, _____and as either pedigreed or non-pedigreed. Seven long-haired breeds and ten short-haired breeds are recognized as pedigreed; cats mated within these breeds will produce offspring with all of the breed's distinguishing characteristics.

2

SIMPLE SENTENCES:

Woodworkers divide wood into two kinds.

One kind is softwood.

The other kind is hardwood.

COMBINATIONS:

(a) _____

(b) _____

(c) _____

(d) _____

(e) _____

CONTEXT:

_____. The first, softwood, comes from trees that bear cones and have needlelike leaves. It is most often used for construction purposes. The second type, hardwood, comes from broad-leafed, flowering trees. It is usually used to build furniture and flooring.

3

SIMPLE SENTENCES:

The ancient Greeks distinguished between two types of drama.

One type was tragic.

The other type was comic.

COMBINATIONS:
(a) _____
(b) _____
(c) _____
(d) _____
(e) _____

CONTEXT:
_____, but they understood these terms differently than we do today. A Greek comedy, for instance, traditionally ended with a scene of sexual revelry, but the play was not necessarily "funny" in the modern sense.

4

Complete the list of simple sentences by filling in the blanks. Then create a set of combinations as before.

SIMPLE SENTENCES:
Psychiatrists divide people into two types.
_____
_____

COMBINATIONS:
(a) _____
(b) _____
(c) _____
(d) _____
(e) _____

OPEN EXERCISE D

The following simple sentences constitute a short essay called "Films as Entertainment." Sentences 48 through 55 are missing; you will have to supply these yourself. (The general topic of the sentences you write should be changes that films are undergoing in the 1980s. Feel free to add more or fewer than the specified number of sentences if you think that doing so will improve the essay.)

Rewrite the sentences in essay form. (A gap between lines indicates that you should start a new paragraph.) You will notice that sentences 6 through 8 are of the type you have worked with in the previous exercise. Some of the sentences you supply should be of this type as well.

Compare your finished essay with those of your classmates and be prepared to discuss the choices you have made.

1. *The Great Train Robbery* was made in 1903.
2. It was the first film to tell a story.
3. It was a silent movie.
4. Silent movies were capable of telling stories.
5. They could do this without creating language barriers.
6. They could be enjoyed by two groups of people.
7. One group was English-speaking people.
8. The other group was non-English-speaking people.
9. Most of the early movie audiences were immigrants.
10. This is a fact.
11. These immigrants could neither read nor write.

12. *The Jazz Singer* was made in 1927.
13. It ended the era of silent movies.
14. Something else happened at about the same time.
15. A new audience began attending movies.
16. This new audience was the middle class.
17. Through the 1930s, there were successful movies.
18. The most successful were of three types.
19. One type was musicals.
20. One such musical was *42nd Street,* made in 1933.
21. Another type was gangster films.
22. One such film was *The Public Enemy,* made in 1931.
23. Still another type was horror movies.
24. One such movie was *Frankenstein,* made in 1931.

25. Television began to compete with movies.
26. It competed as a form of entertainment.
27. This happened in the late 1940s.
28. Movie studios retaliated.
29. This happened in the 1950s.

30. They made more spectacular films.
31. They also began to use new subject matter.
32. This subject matter could not be seen on television.
33. It included nudity and violence.

34. Films from the late 1960s and 1970s were less successful.
35. This was despite the movie studios' efforts.
36. Only a few films made large profits.
37. One of these films was *The Graduate*, made in 1967.
38. Another was *Love Story*, made in 1970.
39. Another was *Rocky*, made in 1976.
40. Another was *Star Wars*, made in 1977.
41. Still another was *Saturday Night Fever*, made in 1977.
42. Films such as these were aimed at a youth audience.
43. This audience becomes increasingly important.

44. Films are being made in the 1980s.
45. They have their own technology.
46. They have their own audiences.
47. And they have their own trends.
48. _____
49. _____
50. _____
51. _____
52. _____
53. _____
54. _____
55. _____
56. One thing is certain, however.
57. Movies of the future may remain a popular entertainment.
58. One thing is necessary if they are to do this.
59. They will have to adapt to changes.
60. These changes are in the world around them.
61. They will have to adapt as movies in the past adapted.

DESCRIPTION

What's strange about the following paragraph?

This section deals with *description;* it contains exercises that will show you tricks and techniques that can add interest to a sentence. You'll learn how to attract attention to ideas by using words and phrases to highlight them. These words and phrases are called modifiers.

Have you figured out why the preceding paragraph sounds a bit odd? It's because all three of its sentences lack just the thing they're talking about: descriptive words and phrases, or *modifiers.* Modifiers add color and detail to a piece of writing. They can describe appearance, number, position in time or space, value, or any other important quality of a person, place, thing, idea, or action. Using modifiers comes so naturally to most writers that it is quite difficult to write a normal-sounding paragraph without them. Here, in contrast, is how the opening paragraph might have looked if some appropriate modifiers had been included:

> This section of the book deals exclusively with *description;* its exercises will show you several tricks and techniques that can make a sentence more interesting. You'll learn how to attract attention to your ideas by using certain types of words and phrases to highlight them. These descriptive words and phrases are, incidentally, called modifiers.

In that one short paragraph, you saw several types of modifiers playing a number of different roles. There were adjectives that described number (**several**), type (**interesting, descriptive**), and possession (**its, your**); prepositional phrases that made a general idea more specific (**of the book, of words and phrases**); and adverbs that modified a single verb (**exclusively**) or an entire sentence (**incidentally**). It's not necessary for you to know what these different kinds of modifiers are called or what each kind does; we've included this example only to give you an idea of the number of ways a modifier can function in a sentence.

You, naturally, will not have to pluck modifiers out of the air as we did in this example. You'll be working, as before, with lists of simple sentences, many of which contain modifiers in disguised forms. The opening paragraph, for instance, included the words **add interest to a sentence;** we later changed this to **make a sentence more interesting.** The two phrases have exactly the same meaning, but the second includes two modifiers (**more** and **interesting**) that were hidden in the first. Likewise, we changed **it contains exercises that will . . .** to **its exercises will . . . ;** the second version, with its modifier **its,** expresses the same idea more neatly. As you do the exercises, you'll discover many more ways in which bulky phrases can be turned into elegant modifiers.

Embedded Modifiers

You will often encounter groups of simple sentences in which one sentence does nothing but modify another. Look, for instance, at the following sentence pairs:

Former Vice President Spiro Agnew wrote a novel.
It was commercially successful.

The Titanic was "unsinkable."
It sank.

Oscar Wilde dismissed criticism of his work.
He did this with scorn.

In the previous section, *Association,* you discovered that you could combine nearly any two related sentences simply by joining them end-to-end. The techniques you used in that section would work equally well here:

Former Vice President Spiro Agnew wrote a novel, and it was commercially successful.

The Titanic was "unsinkable," but it sank.

Oscar Wilde dismissed criticism of his work; he did this with scorn.

There is, however, a much more effective way to combine sentences like these. If you look carefully, you'll find that one of the sentences in each pair can be reduced to one or two important words that modify all or part of the other sentence. Each of these modifiers—**commercially successful,** **"unsinkable,"** and **with scorn**—can be inserted into the other sentence in an appropriate place. This technique, called *embedding,* results in a single, brief sentence that incorporates the meanings of both original sentences. For example:

Former Vice President Spiro Agnew wrote a commercially successful novel.

The "unsinkable" Titanic sank.

Oscar Wilde dismissed criticism of his work with scorn.
[or]
Oscar Wilde scornfully dismissed criticism of his work.

You can see from the third example that there is sometimes more than one way to convert a sentence into a simple modifier. **Scornfully** is a more natural way of saying **with scorn,** and you can use it to create a better-sounding finished sentence. The following set of exercises, all of which require the embedding of modifiers, will give you a chance to try other techniques for reducing an entire sentence to one or two important words.

MODELED EXERCISE A

SIMPLE SENTENCES:
Some people use stoves.
The stoves are wood-burning.

COMBINATIONS:
(a) Some people use wood-burning stoves.
(b) Some people, who use wood-burning stoves, ...
(c) The wood-burning stoves used by some people ...
(d) The stoves used by some people are wood-burning.

Select the combination that works best in the following context.

CONTEXT:
Increased home heating costs have caused a return to older technologies. _____succeed in cutting their fuel bills by more than half.

Now create similar combinations for the following sets of simple sentences. On line e, add your own combination. Then select the one that best fits the given context.

1

SIMPLE SENTENCES:
Many people report seeing flying objects.
The objects are unidentified.

COMBINATIONS:
(a) _____
(b) _____
(c) _____
(d) _____
(e) _____

CONTEXT:
A few UFOs defy explanation, but _____turn out later
to have been meteors.

2

SIMPLE SENTENCES:
Humans have still not explored regions of this planet.
The regions are isolated.

COMBINATIONS:
(a) _____
(b) _____
(c) _____
(d) _____
(e) _____

CONTEXT:
_____. For example, they have not yet seen parts of the
central mountains of New Guinea, nor remote parts of the Brazilian
and African jungles.

3

SIMPLE SENTENCES:
Fine paper requires rags.
The rags must be cotton.

COMBINATIONS:
(a) _____
(b) _____
(c) _____
(d) _____
(e) _____

CONTEXT:
The rags used to make high-quality paper have traditionally come from people's discarded clothing, but only recently has this become a problem for the paper industry. _____are becoming scarce as synthetic clothing grows in popularity.

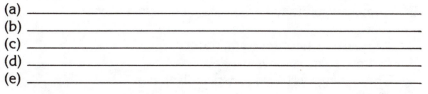

Complete the simple sentence by filling in the blank. Then create a set of combinations as before.

SIMPLE SENTENCES:
Many criminals use handguns.
The handguns are _____.

COMBINATIONS:
(a) _____
(b) _____
(c) _____
(d) _____
(e) _____

OPEN EXERCISE A

The following simple sentences constitute a short essay called "The New American Factory." Rewrite the sentences in essay form. (A gap between lines indicates that you should start a new paragraph.) You will notice that sentences 22–24, 28–29, 33–34, and 39–40 are of the type you have worked with in the previous exercise. Compare your finished essay with those of your classmates and be prepared to discuss the choices you have made.

1. Someday you may be supervising a robot.
2. Someday you may be working alongside a robot.

3. "Increased use of robots is needed.
4. Factory automation is needed.
5. These things will save American factories."
6. That is said by some people.
7. Many American factories are outdated.
8. "Some of my plants are extremely outdated.
9. They make Santa's Workshop look like the factory of the future."
10. One top industry executive admits this.
11. Foreign products have been attracting consumers.
12. Their prices are lower.
13. Their quality is higher.
14. Consumers have turned increasingly to imported goods.
15. Some of the goods are Japanese.
16. Some are from other nations.
17. America must compete.
18. It must update its old factories for that reason.
19. It must find a way to achieve lower costs.
20. It must find a way to achieve higher quality.

21. Already, robots are used in factories.
22. Robots replace people on jobs.
23. The jobs may be repetitive.
24. The jobs may be dangerous.
25. Some robots paint.
26. They are not bothered by spray paint fumes.
27. Some robots weld.
28. They make the same welds 24 hours a day.
29. The welds are monotonous.
30. The robots do not mind this.

31. Traditionally, workers have protested automation.
32. They have seen it as a change.
33. The change would eliminate jobs.
34. The jobs are needed.
35. Now, American industry must be updated.
36. Many workers now realize this.
37. Automation will cost some jobs.

38. The jobs will be here and there.
39. A business failure can empty a factory.
40. The factory may be huge.
41. It may be emptied in a day.
42. The workers understand these things.

43. "Economic conditions for some companies may be poor.
44. Nevertheless, they should buy new equipment now.
45. They should not wait until times are better."
46. That is what experts say.
47. "There is a choice.
48. You can bite the bullet.
49. Or you can bite the dust."
50. That is what one expert says.

MODELED EXERCISE B

SIMPLE SENTENCES:
Acid rain is a problem.
The problem is growing.

COMBINATIONS:
(a) Acid rain is a growing problem.
(b) The acid rain problem is growing.
(c) Acid rain is growing as a problem.
(d) The growing problem of acid rain . . .

Select the combination that works best in the following context.

CONTEXT:
_____has led to the death of the fish populations of 3,000 Adirondack lakes. Acid rain is probably caused by sulfur dioxide blown from the industries of the Ohio Valley.

Now create similar combinations for the following sets of simple sentences. On line e, add your own combination. Then select the one that best fits the given context.

1

SIMPLE SENTENCES:
Flextime is a technique.
The technique is humanizing.

COMBINATIONS:
(a) _____
(b) _____
(c) _____
(d) _____
(e) _____

CONTEXT:
There have been several recent attempts to make workers feel less regimented. Flextime is one such attempt, and it has met with considerable success. _____that allows workers to set their own hours, within certain limits. Apart from its advantages to the individual worker, flextime can benefit the entire community by cutting down the number of commuters who travel during the peak rush hours.

2

SIMPLE SENTENCES:
The Ferris Wheel was a structure.
The structure was amazing.

COMBINATIONS:
(a) _____
(b) _____
(c) _____
(d) _____
(e) _____

CONTEXT:
Intended as a direct competitor to the Eiffel Tower of the 1889 Paris Expositions, _____ 250 feet tall. As was hoped by its inventor, Gale Ferris, it soon became the symbol of the 1893 World's Fair in Chicago.

3

SIMPLE SENTENCES:
Health statistics are an argument.
The argument is compelling.

COMBINATIONS:
(a) _____
(b) _____
(c) _____
(d) _____
(e) _____

CONTEXT:
People say that none of the arguments for the 1969 Clean Air Act is justified, but _____: thanks to cleaner air, health groups have estimated that each American's life span is one year longer.

4

Complete the simple sentence by filling in the blank. Then create a set of combinations as before.

SIMPLE SENTENCES:
_____will be a disaster.
The disaster will be overwhelming.

COMBINATIONS:
(a) _____
(b) _____
(c) _____
(d) _____
(e) _____

OPEN EXERCISE B

The following simple sentences constitute a short essay called "The Giant Hoax." Rewrite the sentences in essay form. (A gap between lines indicates that you should start a new paragraph.) You will notice that sentences 11–12, 29–30, and 42–43 are of the type you have worked with in the previous exercise. Compare your finished essay with those of your classmates and be prepared to discuss the choices you have made.

1. Things are not always what they seem.
2. This is so even in the world of archaeology.
3. That world is respected.
4. In 1869 a ten-foot giant was unearthed in a field.
5. The giant was stone.
6. The field was a farmer's.
7. The field was in Cardiff, New York.
8. The giant was proclaimed to be a petrified man.
9. It was proclaimed to be a relic of prehistoric times.
10. This proclamation was made immediately.
11. But behind the "discovery" was a farmer.
12. The farmer was fast-talking.
13. Also behind the "discovery" were the farmer's accomplices.

14. The discovery became known as the Cardiff giant.
15. It was the brainchild of George Hull and a partner.
16. George Hull and his partner had hired sculptors.
17. The sculptors were to carve the statue.
18. Hull poured sulfuric acid over the statue.
19. He did this when the statue was completed.
20. The acid gave the statue a more aged look.
21. The figure was then shipped to the farm of Hull's friend.
22. Hull's friend was William C. Newell.
23. Newell buried the statue behind his barn.
24. The statue lay behind the barn for about a year.
25. Newell hired workmen in October 1869.
26. The workmen were to dig a well on the spot.
27. The workmen were unsuspecting.
28. They dug deeper.
29. Eventually, the form of the giant was seen.
30. The form was emerging.
31. Word of the "prehistoric discovery" spread quickly.
32. Soon Newell was charging 50 cents admission.

33. Two thousand people came each weekend.

34. Hull was crafty.
35. Hull knew he must sell the giant before his plot was exposed.
36. A week passed after the giant was discovered.
37. Hull sold a three-quarter interest in the statue.
38. He sold it for $30,000.
39. People suspected that the figure was a hoax.
40. Their suspicions were intensifying.
41. In spite of this, crowds continued to visit the figure.
42. Finally, Hull could no longer deny the evidence.
43. The evidence was mounting.
44. It was December.
45. Hull admitted the hoax.
46. But the statue still drew crowds.

47. The Cardiff giant is still on view.
48. It is at the Farmer's Museum in Cooperstown, New York.
49. It is no longer seen as an archaeological relic.
50. It is seen as something intriguing.
51. It is seen as a curiosity from America's past.

MODELED EXERCISE C

SIMPLE SENTENCES:
The marijuana was harvested.
The growers sold it.
They anticipated a crackdown.

COMBINATIONS:
(a) The growers, anticipating a crackdown, sold the harvested marijuana.
(b) The harvested marijuana was sold by the growers, who anticipated a crackdown.
(c) Anticipating a crackdown, the growers sold the marijuana that was harvested.
(d) The marijuana was harvested; the growers, who anticipated a crackdown, sold it.

Select the combination that works best in the following context.

CONTEXT:
News of a renewed war on drugs by the Reagan administration had little effect on the 1982 marijuana crop. _____more cheaply—and therefore more quickly—than they might have otherwise. In spite of this pressure, they made very large profits. As of 1982, marijuana was the nation's fourth largest cash crop.

Now create similar combinations for the following sets of simple sentences. On line e, add your own combination. Then select the one that best fits the given context.

1

SIMPLE SENTENCES:
The novel was reprinted.
A mistake marred it.
The mistake was unnoticed for many years.

COMBINATIONS:
(a) _____
(b) _____
(c) _____
(d) _____
(e) _____

CONTEXT:
Henry James's *The Ambassadors,* first published in England, was reissued in the United States by Harper and Brothers. _____ _____, which nonetheless met with critical acclaim. Chapter 29 was accidentally printed ahead of Chapter 28.

2

SIMPLE SENTENCES:
A women's college was proposed.
Mary Lyon established it.
She recognized the value of an education.

COMBINATIONS:
(a) _____
(b) _____

(c) _____
(d) _____
(e) _____

CONTEXT:
There was a feeling among many people in the early nineteenth century that women should have the same educational advantages as men. _____. She presided over the college—called Mount Holyoke Seminary—until her death in 1849.

3

SIMPLE SENTENCES:
The children were orphaned.
The French state supported them.
It responded to Napoleon's wishes.

COMBINATIONS:
(a) _____
(b) _____
(c) _____
(d) _____
(e) _____

CONTEXT:
Many French children lost their fathers at the battle of Austerlitz, but Napoleon did not neglect them. _____and provided for their education. The emperor himself adopted them, allowing them to add his own name, *Napoleon,* to theirs.

4

Complete the simple sentences by filling in the blanks. Then create a set of combinations as before.

SIMPLE SENTENCES:
My schoolwork was finished.
_____ate it.
[S]he _____.

COMBINATIONS:

(a) _____

(b) _____

(c) _____

(d) _____

(e) _____

OPEN EXERCISE C

The following simple sentences constitute a short essay called "A Life Lived In a Circle." Rewrite the sentences in essay form. (A gap between lines indicates that you should start a new paragraph.) You will notice that sentences 28–30 and 61–63 are of the type you have worked with in the previous exercise. Compare your finished essay with those of your classmates and be prepared to discuss the choices you have made.

1. The life of Ferdinand Magellan is full of paradoxes.
2. The paradoxes are strange.
3. He helped Portugal to conquer the Spice Islands.
4. Then he proved that they belonged to Spain.
5. He had sailed around the world.
6. He was the first man to do this.
7. Yet he died in the middle of a voyage.
8. That voyage confirmed that the world was round.
9. He sailed halfway around the world as a Portuguese citizen.
10. He was working for the king of Portugal.
11. He sailed the other half as an exile.
12. He was working for the king of Spain.

13. At the start of the sixteenth century Portugal was a great exploring power.
14. At the start of the sixteenth century Spain was a great exploring power.
15. They had made an agreement.
16. They would divide the world between them.
17. The Spanish half would be to the west.
18. The Portuguese half would be to the east.
19. Magellan was a volunteer with the Portuguese fleet.
20. That fleet explored the East Indies.

21. That fleet conquered the East Indies.
22. The East Indies included the Spice Islands.
23. The Spice Islands were desirable.
24. Magellan developed a plan.
25. His plan was to find a westward route to the Spice Islands.
26. He returned to Portugal.
27. There, he fell into disfavor with the king.

28. Magellan was exiled.
29. Spain welcomed him.
30. Spain was the rival of Portugal.
31. The king of Spain listened to Magellan's ideas.
32. "The Spice Islands can be reached from the west.
33. They might be in the Spanish half of the world.
34. They might not be in the Portuguese half."
35. That was Magellan's argument.
36. He obtained five boats.
37. He had less than 300 men.
38. He set sail for South America.
39. He wanted to find a passage.
40. The passage would go through that continent.

41. He searched down the coast of South America.
42. He searched many bays.
43. He searched many rivers.
44. He finally happened upon a passage.
45. The passage separates Tierra del Fuego from the mainland.
46. It is now called the Strait of Magellan.
47. He sailed through.
48. He sailed into the Pacific.
49. He sailed for 100 days on the open sea.
50. He sighted Guam.
51. He sailed on to the Philippines.
52. There he died in a local battle.

53. The Philippines are west of the Spice Islands.
54. The Spice Islands could be reached by a westward route.
55. Magellan had shown that.
56. He had also shown that they were in the Spanish half of the world.
57. Finally, he had circled the world.

58. He had sailed back from the Spice Islands with the Portuguese fleet.
59. Later, he had reached the Philippines for the king of Spain.

60. One of Magellan's achievements did not last long.
61. The Spice Islands were newly gained.
62. The Spanish sold them.
63. They foresaw difficulty in reaching them.
64. The Strait of Magellan was an impractical route.
65. The islands were sold to Portugal.
66. This was ironic.

MODELED EXERCISE D

SIMPLE SENTENCES:
The Egyptians preserved their dead.
The preservation was ingenious.
They used the process of mummification.

COMBINATIONS:
(a) The Egyptians ingeniously preserved their dead by using the process of mummification.
(b) The Egyptians, using the process of mummification, ingeniously preserved their dead.
(c) Ingeniously using the process of mummification, the Egyptians preserved their dead.
(d) The Egyptians' preservation of their dead was ingenious: they used the process of mummification.

Select the combination that works best in the following context.

CONTEXT:
A significant difference between the ancient Egyptian and the Greek civilizations is seen in their burial practices. _____. They believed that without a body there could be no afterlife. The Greeks, who commonly used funeral pyres and cremation, destroyed their dead. They believed that the soul and the body were separate.

Now create similar combinations for the following sets of simple sentences. On line e, add your own combination. Then select the one that best fits the given context.

1

SIMPLE SENTENCES:
Jean François Champollion translated the Rosetta Stone.
The translation was successful.
He used a new approach.

COMBINATIONS:
(a) _____
(b) _____
(c) _____
(d) _____
(e) _____

CONTEXT:
When, _____, a vast new area of ancient history was opened to us. The stone provided the key to understanding Egyptian hieroglyphics. All the ancient inscriptions could now be read and understood.

2

SIMPLE SENTENCES:
The Grimke sisters campaigned against slavery.
The campaign was vehement.
They wrote many antislavery pamphlets.

COMBINATIONS:
(a) _____
(b) _____
(c) _____
(d) _____
(e) _____

CONTEXT:
Daughters of a slave owner, _____and by addressing meetings with their views on abolition. They were among the first respectable American women to speak in public, and doubtless some of their audience came to see them as a spectacle.

3

SIMPLE SENTENCES:
Charles Goodyear discovered vulcanized rubber.
The discovery was accidental.
He dropped a mixture of rubber and sulfur onto a hot stove.

COMBINATIONS:
(a) _____
(b) _____
(c) _____
(d) _____
(e) _____

CONTEXT:
Invention is often a mixture of luck and hard work—witness the development of heat-resistant qualities in rubber. _____.
However, his development of this discovery for commercial use was
painstaking. Goodyear worked on the process for some time before
he felt it was ready to be patented.

4

*Complete the simple sentences by filling in the blanks. Then create
a set of combinations as before.*

SIMPLE SENTENCES:
Many young teenagers express their devotion to _____.
The expression is _____.
They go out of their way to _____.

COMBINATIONS:
(a) _____
(b) _____
(c) _____
(d) _____
(e) _____

OPEN EXERCISE D

*The following simple sentences constitute a short essay called "Early
Opposition to the Draft." Sentences 10 through 17 are missing; you
will have to supply these yourself. (The general topic of the sentences*

you write should be how or why young people have recently expressed their opposition to draft registration. Feel free to add more or fewer than the specified number of sentences if you think that doing so will improve the essay.)

Rewrite the sentences in essay form. (A gap between lines indicates that you should start a new paragraph.) You will notice that sentences 37–39 and 45–47 are of the type you have worked with in the previous exercise. Some of the sentences you supply should be of this type as well.

Compare your finished essay with those of your classmates and be prepared to discuss the choices you have made.

1. Draft registration returned in 1979.
2. It revived a spirit of rebellion.
3. The spirit was in America's young people.
4. It had lain dormant for nearly a decade.
5. Young men and women expressed their opposition.
6. They did this through words and actions.
7. Their opposition was to the draft.
8. Their oppposition was to war in general.
9. They began to express it once again.
10. _____
11. _____
12. _____
13. _____
14. _____
15. _____
16. _____
17. _____

18. There is opposition to the draft.
19. It is not limited to recent years.
20. The military draft has faced opposition since its birth.
21. The Civil War was in progress.
22. The need for Union soldiers was growing.
23. This need led Congress to pass an act.
24. It was called the Enrollment Act.
25. It was the country's first national draft law.
26. It was passed on March 3, 1863.

27. Able-bodied white men had to register with the government.
28. These men were between the ages of 20 and 45.
29. They were subject to three years of military service.
30. The physically unfit were exempted.
31. The only sons of dependent parents were exempted.
32. High federal and state officials were exempted.
33. Drafted men could do two things.
34. They could provide a substitute.
35. They could pay the government $300.
36. This would buy an exemption.
37. Many people protested the exemption clause.
38. Their protests were violent.
39. They joined riots.
40. Draft riots occurred in many northern cities.
41. However, New York City's riots were by far the worst.
42. Most of New York's draft eligibles were Irish laborers.
43. They were too poor to buy their exemptions.

44. It was July 11, 1863.
45. The New York authorities selected draftees.
46. The selection was quiet.
47. They used a random lottery.
48. The next day over 1,200 names were listed.
49. Then came Monday, July 13.
50. Small groups of people left their homes.
51. These groups were of men, women, and children.
52. Their homes were mostly tenements.
53. They were armed with crowbars, clubs, and brickbats.
54. They converged at the draft office.
55. The office was on Third Avenue.
56. They were soon joined by thieves.
57. They were joined by other criminals.
58. All wanted some action.
59. The group showered the building with bricks and stones.
60. Spectators urged them on.
61. They forced their way into the building.
62. They shredded books, records, and lists.
63. They set the building on fire.
64. By noon, 50,000 rioters filled Third Avenue.
65. They looted homes and stores.

66. At one point a rifle factory was burned.
67. The fire trapped many of the rioters.
68. It killed many of them.

69. By nightfall, the violence was no longer limited to one area.
70. It was scattered throughout the city.
71. The police did what they could.
72. The governor of New York urged the rioters to stop.
73. Two days passed.
74. Thirteen army regiments came to the city.
75. Only then did the turmoil end.
76. Over 1,000 people were killed in the draft riot.
77. The riot was one of the most destructive riots in American history.

Free Modifiers

The exercises you've completed so far in this section have dealt with very simple sorts of modifiers. Most of the modifiers were made up of no more than a word or two, and could only be placed right next to the word or phrase they were modifying. There is, however, another kind of modifier used commonly in writing. It is called a *free modifier,* and, as its name implies, it can be placed nearly anywhere in the sentence it modifies: at the beginning, in the middle, or at the end. Free modifiers are somewhat more complicated than ordinary modifiers, but they do an equally good job of description. Look, for example, at the following pair of sentences:

Jimmy Carter delivered his concession speech.
His eyes were moist with tears.

The second sentence clearly modifies the first, but, unlike the sentences you worked with earlier, it cannot be reduced to a word or two. (Since **moist** describes Carter's eyes rather than Carter himself, **his eyes** must also be included if the modifier is to make sense.) As a result, the entire second sentence—with one minor change to convert it into a phrase—becomes a modifier. And because it is so nearly a sentence itself, it can act much more independently than the simpler modifiers you have dealt with so far. Here are some possible combinations:

His eyes moist with tears, Jimmy Carter delivered his concession speech.

Jimmy Carter, his eyes moist with tears, delivered his concession speech.

Jimmy Carter delivered his concession speech, his eyes moist with tears.

Of course, it is not absolutely necessary to convert the second sentence into a free modifier. You still have the option of combining the two sentences in some of the ways we talked about in the **Association** section. Here, then, are some more possible combinations:

As Jimmy Carter delivered his concession speech, his eyes were moist with tears.

His eyes were moist with tears as Jimmy Carter delivered his concession speech.

Jimmy Carter delivered his concession speech; his eyes were moist with tears.

There are several different kinds of free modifiers. (The type we have worked with here is called an **absolute,** but technical words aren't important for our purposes.) You'll be working with these different types in the following exercises, and you'll have a chance to see how each different kind of free modifier behaves. You may find these exercises a bit more difficult than those you worked on earlier in this section, but you won't run into any real problems if you follow the models closely. Careful imitation now will lead to greater freedom in writing later on.

MODELED EXERCISE A

SIMPLE SENTENCES:
Boston colonists rebelled in December 1773.
They rebelled by raiding ships in the harbor.

COMBINATIONS:
(a) Raiding ships in the harbor, Boston colonists rebelled in December 1773.
(b) Boston colonists rebelled, raiding ships in the harbor, in December 1773.
(c) Boston colonists rebelled in December 1773, raiding ships in the harbor.
(d) Boston colonists, raiding ships in the harbor, rebelled in December 1773.

Select the combination that works best in the following context.

CONTEXT:
Throughout the American colonies, the tea tax became a symbol of British tyranny. _____and throwing 342 chests of tea overboard.

Now create similar combinations for the following sets of simple sentences. On line e, add your own combination. Then select the one that best fits the given context.

1

SIMPLE SENTENCES:
Spaceships can travel on reflected light.
They can travel by using mirror sails.

COMBINATIONS:
(a) _____
(b) _____
(c) _____
(d) _____
(e) _____

CONTEXT:
Light reflecting off a mirror actually exerts pressure on the mirror. In space, there is no atmosphere to resist this pressure. Therefore, it is possible—at least in theory—that _____for great distances without any fuel.

2

SIMPLE SENTENCES:
The poet John Keats died at age 25.
He died believing he was a failure.

COMBINATIONS:
(a) _____
(b) _____
(c) _____
(d) _____
(e) _____

CONTEXT:
In 1821, _____from stomach cancer. He had no way
to know that his odes and sonnets would someday be regarded as
masterpieces.

3

SIMPLE SENTENCES:
Mexico was the home of a series of powerful civilizations.
It was their home beginning in 1200 B.C.

COMBINATIONS:
(a) _____
(b) _____
(c) _____
(d) _____
(e) _____

CONTEXT:
For nearly 3,000 years, _____: the Olmecs, the Mayas,
and then the Aztecs.

4

*Complete the simple sentence by filling in the blank. Then create a
set of combinations as before.*

SIMPLE SENTENCES:
The Soviet Union competes with the United States.
It competes by _____.

COMBINATIONS:
(a) _____
(b) _____
(c) _____
(d) _____
(e) _____

OPEN EXERCISE A

The following simple sentences constitute a short essay called "Left-Handed Life." Rewrite the sentences in essay form. (A gap between lines indicates that you should start a new paragraph.) You will notice that sentences 16–17 and 42–44 are of the type you have worked with in the previous exercise. Compare your finished essay with those of your classmates and be prepared to discuss the choices you have made.

1. Life isn't easy for some people.
2. These people are left-handed.
3. You may be a lefty.
4. In that case, you are familiar with the frustration.
5. The frustration comes from using certain things.
6. Right-handed scissors are one of these things.
7. Can openers are another.
8. The typewriter is one rare machine.
9. Its keyboard has letters on the left-hand side.
10. Those letters are the most commonly used.
11. Most other appliances are designed for right-handed users.
12. Cameras are in this category.
13. Automobiles are in this category.
14. Telephones are in this category.
15. Even pinball machines are in this category.
16. Most lefties learn to adapt to a right-handed world.
17. They adapt by becoming almost ambidextrous.

18. One can play sports left-handed.
19. This can be an advantage in some sports.
20. Athletes have to face opponents.
21. Some opponents lead from the left side.
22. Most athletes aren't accustomed to facing these opponents.
23. This is an advantage in any one-on-one competition.
24. Tennis is in this category.
25. Boxing is in this category.
26. Fencing is in this category.
27. Baseball can also be in this category.
28. This is the case when pitchers face batters.
29. Left-handedness is not so important in other sports.
30. Golf is one of these sports.
31. Bowling is another one.
32. Players compete in these sports only by scoring.
33. It is against the rules to play one sport left-handed.
34. This sport is polo.
35. Something would happen otherwise.
36. The polo ponies would run into each other.
37. They would be doing this constantly.

38. You may be a musician.
39. In that case, being left-handed doesn't matter much.
40. There is a reason for this.
41. Most instruments require both hands to play.
42. Some guitarists play left-handed.
43. They play by turning their guitars around.
44. They play by restringing their guitars.
45. Violinists are not allowed to play on the opposite side.
46. One violin bow might move in the opposite direction.
47. This would cause something to happen in an orchestra.
48. Can you imagine what?
49. These are problems.
50. They are the sorts lefties learn to live with.

MODELED EXERCISE B

SIMPLE SENTENCES:

Mt. St. Helens is a volcano of only moderate size.
It erupted with considerable violence.
This was a reminder of man's powerlessness against nature.

COMBINATIONS:
(a) A volcano of only moderate size, Mt. St. Helens erupted with considerable violence, a reminder of man's powerlessness against nature.
(b) Mt. St. Helens is a volcano of only moderate size that erupted with considerable violence—a reminder of man's powerlessness against nature.
(c) It was a reminder of man's powerlessness against nature when Mt. St. Helens, a volcano of only moderate size, erupted with considerable violence.
(d) Mt. St. Helens, a volcano of only moderate size, erupted with considerable violence, a reminder of man's powerlessness against nature.

Select the combination that works best in the following context.

CONTEXT:
Realistically speaking, _____. However, that violence was relatively minor. In Southern Oregon, some 7,000 years ago, the explosion of a volcano left a crater six miles wide. The ash from that explosion traveled as far as Saskatchewan, Canada.

Now create similar combinations for the following sets of simple sentences. On line e, add your own combination. Then select the one that best fits the given context.

1

SIMPLE SENTENCES:
Luciano Pavarotti is a singer of superb talent.
He catapulted opera into the spotlight of the media.
This was a feat of no mean proportions.

COMBINATIONS:
(a) _____
(b) _____
(c) _____
(d) _____
(e) _____

CONTEXT:
_____, the news weeklies in particular. In a sense, he has done for opera what Pelé did for American soccer.

2

SIMPLE SENTENCES:
Alfred Nobel was a philanthropist of considerable generosity.
He turned his entire fortune into a fund for international prizes.
This was an act of enduring significance.

COMBINATIONS:
(a) _____
(b) _____
(c) _____
(d) _____
(e) _____

CONTEXT:
Showing himself to be _____. The fortune had resulted
from Nobel's experiments with nitroglycerin, which led to patents for
dynamite and other important explosives.

3

SIMPLE SENTENCES:
The Mediterranean fruitfly is a warm-weather insect.
It poses little threat to northern orchards.
This is a welcome fact about an otherwise unwelcome pest.

COMBINATIONS:
(a) _____
(b) _____
(c) _____
(d) _____
(e) _____

CONTEXT:
_____under normal weather conditions. However, a long,
hot summer might enable them to make inroads further north.

4

*Complete the simple sentences by filling in the blanks. Then create
a set of combinations as before.*

SIMPLE SENTENCES:

I am a believer in _____.

I want to _____.

It will be a major breakthrough in my search for _____.

COMBINATIONS:

(a) _____

(b) _____

(c) _____

(d) _____

(e) _____

OPEN EXERCISE B

The following simple sentences constitute a short essay called "Light and Behavior." Rewrite the sentences in essay form. (A gap between lines indicates that you should start a new paragraph.) You will notice that sentences 17 through 19 are of the type you have worked with in the previous exercise. Compare your finished essay with those of your classmates and be prepared to discuss the choices you have made.

1. Animals have daily rhythms.
2. These rhythms are often synchronized with the time of day.
3. Scientists have long known this.
4. They also know the following.
5. Changes in the amount of sunlight have an effect.
6. They cue various seasonal activities.
7. These include many things.
8. One example is spring growth in plants.
9. Another example is the mating season in animals.
10. There can be other things as well.
11. Farmers know that seasonal behavior can be controlled.
12. It can be controlled by using light.
13. Farmers have put this knowledge to good use.
14. There is an example.
15. Egg production in chickens increases in spring.
16. This is because the days grow longer.
17. Artificial light is used by farmers to lengthen the day.

18. It can make chickens behave as if it were spring.
19. This is an effective technique for increasing egg production.

20. Researchers have made a number of discoveries.
21. The discoveries have occurred in recent years.
22. They reveal connections.
23. The connections are between light and health.
24. The connections are new and unexpected.
25. The researchers are learning about the following things.
26. All aspects of health are affected by the light we are exposed to.
27. One aspect is physical health.
28. Another aspect is mental health.
29. Still another aspect is emotional health.
30. These things are affected by the intensity of the light.
31. They are affected by the amount of exposure to the light.
32. They are affected by the color of the light.

33. Scientists have a concern.
34. The concern is about the effects of artificial light.
35. Humans spend time in artificial light.
36. They spend more time than they used to.
37. They do not spend as much time in natural light.
38. Artificial light differs from natural light.
39. It differs in character.
40. It differs in intensity.
41. This difference has results.
42. Scientists are just beginning to understand the results.
43. Fluorescent light is the chief source of concern.
44. It is not like natural light.
45. It does not contain a wide spectrum of colors.
46. Natural light contains a wide spectrum of colors.
47. The colors have a range.
48. Ultraviolet is at one end of the range.
49. Visible light is in the middle.
50. Infrared light is at the other end.
51. Fluorescent light has a limited spectrum.
52. It is particularly limited in two ranges.
53. One is the ultraviolet range.
54. One is the blue-green range.
55. Sunlight is most intense in the blue-green range.

56.   These limits may have an effect.
57.   They may cause depression.
58.   They may cause sleep disorders.
59.   They may cause fatigue.
60.   These things may occur in people who are exposed to this light.

MODELED EXERCISE C

SIMPLE SENTENCES:
The Arctic tern is unique among migratory birds.
It travels from pole to pole twice each year.
It exploits summer at both poles.

COMBINATIONS:
(a)   Unique among migratory birds, the Arctic tern travels from pole
      to pole twice each year, exploiting summer at both poles.
(b)   The Arctic tern is unique among migratory birds: it travels from
      pole to pole twice each year, exploiting summer at both poles.
(c)   The Arctic tern, unique among migratory birds, travels from pole
      to pole twice each year and exploits summer at both poles.
(d)   Traveling from pole to pole twice each year and exploiting summer
      at both poles, the Arctic tern is unique among migratory birds.

Select the combination that works best in the following context.

CONTEXT:
_____of both hemispheres. Its round-trip journey is
25,000 miles each year.

Now create similar combinations for the following sets of simple sentences. On line e, add your own combination. Then select the one that best fits the given context.

1

SIMPLE SENTENCES:
Mozart was musically mature beyond his years.
He performed in public from age six onward.
He delighted audiences at the courts of Europe.

COMBINATIONS:

(a) _____

(b) _____

(c) _____

(d) _____

(e) _____

CONTEXT:

_____, doing both with an easy grace all his own. His courtly manners were charming—it is said that he assured Marie Antoinette he would marry her when he grew up.

2

SIMPLE SENTENCES:

Bob Beamon's long jump record is improbable in its sheer magnitude.
His long jump record has easily withstood all challenges so far.
It looks ever more like a superhuman achievement.

COMBINATIONS:

(a) _____

(b) _____

(c) _____

(d) _____

(e) _____

CONTEXT:

It is not just another record to be broken before long; at 29 feet, 2½ inches, _____.

3

SIMPLE SENTENCES:

Mt. Kilimanjaro is serene in its snowcapped majesty.
It rises from the steppes of East Africa.
It dominates the surrounding landscape.

COMBINATIONS:

(a) _____

(b) _____

(c) _____
(d) _____
(e) _____

CONTEXT:
Stately and _____. At over 19,000 feet it is the highest
mountain on the African continent.

4

Complete the simple sentence by filling in the blank. Then create a
set of combinations as before.

SIMPLE SENTENCES:
The Beatles were unusual among rock groups.
They brought many new sounds into the world of pop music.
They _____.

COMBINATIONS:
(a) _____
(b) _____
(c) _____
(d) _____
(e) _____

OPEN EXERCISE C

The following simple sentences constitute a short essay called "The
Fuel-Efficient Horse." Rewrite the sentences in essay form. (A gap
between lines indicates that you should start a new paragraph.) You
will notice that sentences 3–5 and 13–15 are of the type you have
worked with in the previous exercise. Compare your finished essay
with those of your classmates and be prepared to discuss the choices
you have made.

1. A horse may be in motion.
2. It gradually picks up speed.
3. The horse is like an automobile.
4. It will shift from "low gear" to "high gear."

5.   It changes from a walk to a trot to a gallop.
6.   A primary factor determines when these "gear shifts" take place.
7.   That factor is speed.
8.   This can be demonstrated by conducting an experiment.
9.   The experiment is simple.
10.   Horses can be trained to run in place.
11.   They run on a treadmill.
12.   The treadmill is motorized.
13.   The experimenters are careful to observe changes in the horses' gaits.
14.   They turn up the dial.
15.   They increase the treadmill's speed.
16.   The increase in speed will have a result.
17.   The horses will change gaits.
18.   The changes are consistent.
19.   They happen at about the same speeds.

20.   Two researchers investigated the reason for this phenomenon.
21.   The predictibility of the gait changes intrigued them.
22.   They guessed that one principle would lie at the heart of the matter.
23.   That principle is energy efficiency.
24.   The researchers measured horses' consumption of oxygen.
25.   They did this with gas masks.
26.   The gas masks were custom-made.
27.   The researchers made an observation.
28.   They found that the faster a horse runs, the more energy it burns.
29.   This is not the whole story.
30.   If it were, little of interest would have been learned.
31.   It turns out that there is more to the story.
32.   The experimenters discovered something else.
33.   A horse's energy consumption increases as its speed increases.
34.   This happens most of the time.
35.   But something else happens at certain times.
36.   The horse's energy consumption levels off.
37.   Then it increases more slowly.
38.   This happens when the horse's gait changes.
39.   A conclusion can be reached from this.
40.   It is that gait changes are a way of remaining energy efficient.
41.   Other evidence supports this conclusion.

42. A horse can be trained to use a gallop at a certain time.
43. A walk would be normal at this time.
44. A horse can be trained to use a trot at a certain time.
45. A gallop would be normal at this time.
46. The horse's gait does not match its speed.
47. This has a result.
48. The result is that the horse expends energy.
49. The energy is more than would be expended normally.
50. Normally, the horse uses a gait appropriate to its speed.
51. Using an inappropriate gait is similar to some other things.
52. It is like trying to race in low gear.
53. It is like trying to inch along in high gear.
54. In so doing, the horse fights basic laws.
55. The laws govern the mechanics of motion.

MODELED EXERCISE D

SIMPLE SENTENCES:
The Huns overran much of Europe.
They were persistent in battle.
They were unrivaled as horsemen.

COMBINATIONS:
(a) The Huns, persistent in battle and unrivaled as horsemen, overran much of Europe.
(b) Persistent in battle and unrivaled as horsemen, the Huns overran much of Europe.
(c) The Huns overran much of Europe, persistent in battle and unrivaled as horsemen.
(d) In overrunning much of Europe, the Huns were persistent in battle and unrivaled as horsemen.

Select the combination that works best in the following context.

CONTEXT:
Stubbornly _____. They might have invaded China as well if the Chinese had not erected the Great Wall to keep them out.

Now create similar combinations for the following sets of simple sentences. On line e, add your own combination. Then select the one that best fits the given context.

1

SIMPLE SENTENCES:
The other bees navigate by the sun.
They are efficient.
They are skilled at learning new routes.

COMBINATIONS:
(a) _____
(b) _____
(c) _____
(d) _____
(e) _____

CONTEXT:
When a bee finds a new stand of flowers, it returns to the hive and communicates directions by performing a "dance." _____
_____to locate the flowers in a remarkably short time.

2

SIMPLE SENTENCES:
Schubert set aside the symphony he had been writing.
He was ill with typhoid.
He was overcome with frustration.

COMBINATIONS:
(a) _____
(b) _____
(c) _____
(d) _____
(e) _____

CONTEXT:
_____at the work's slow progress. He later recovered from his illness, but he never returned to the symphony; it is known today as the *Unfinished.*

3

SIMPLE SENTENCES:
Insects adapt to new habitats.
They are free of natural enemies.
They are aided by their own versatility.

COMBINATIONS:
(a) _____
(b) _____
(c) _____
(d) _____
(e) _____

CONTEXT:
Outside of an insect's natural habitat, predators are unlikely to recognize it as a potential meal. Therefore, _____in finding
new sources of food.

4

*Complete the simple sentences by filling in the blanks. Then create
a set of combinations as before.*

SIMPLE SENTENCES:
I frequently delay doing _____.
I am _____.
I am _____.

COMBINATIONS:
(a) _____
(b) _____
(c) _____
(d) _____
(e) _____

OPEN EXERCISE D

*The following simple sentences constitute a short essay called "A
Closer Look at the Telephone." Sentences 29 through 38 are missing;
you will have to supply these yourself. (The general topic of the sen-*

tences you write should be a problem people encounter when they try to communicate over the telephone. Feel free to add more or fewer than the specified number of sentences if you think that doing so will improve the essay.)

Rewrite the sentences in essay form. (A gap between lines indicates that you should start a new paragraph.) You will notice that sentences 1–3 and 62–64 are of the type you have worked with in the previous exercise. Some of the sentences you supply should be of this type as well.

Compare your finished essay with those of your classmates and be prepared to discuss the choices you have made.

1. The telephone is a part of modern life.
2. It is emotionally neutral.
3. It is always available.
4. That it is so much a part of life has a result.
5. The result is that people do not think about the telephone.
6. People do not take the time.
7. The telephone is everywhere.
8. It is at our disposal.
9. We are content with that.
10. We simply use the telephone.
11. We use it for every form of human communication.
12. We take the telephone for granted.
13. But we have feelings about it.
14. The feelings are definite.

15. This was shown in a series of interviews.
16. The series was recent.
17. The interviews were with residents of a Canadian city.
18. Most of these people sense the limitations of the telephone.
19. This is so even though the people depend on it.
20. Many people said that the telephone feels impersonal.
21. Others expressed dissatisfaction with their own ability.
22. Their ability is to communicate effectively over the telephone.
23. Still others felt that the telephone presents a problem.
24. The problem is severe.

25. The problem is that the telephone cannot let them see the other person.
26. The person is the one to whom they are speaking.
27. Of all these limitations, one is especially significant.
28. It causes problems for many people.
29. _____
30. _____
31. _____
32. _____
33. _____
34. _____
35. _____
36. _____
37. _____
38. _____

39. These impressions may be valid.
40. However, there is a solid body of evidence.
41. The evidence has been accumulated over the last decade.
42. It suggests that the telephone has definite advantages.
43. The advantages are over face-to-face conversation.
44. This is so in certain situations.
45. These situations have something in common.
46. It is that one person tries to change attitudes.
47. The attitudes are held by the other person.
48. The following has been shown.
49. In negotiations, one person has a stronger case.
50. The other person has a weaker case.
51. The first person has a better chance of convincing the second.
52. The chance is better over the phone than in a face-to-face encounter.
53. Another finding is just as intriguing.
54. It is that people are less easily deceived on the phone.
55. It is that people are less easily manipulated on the phone.
56. They are more easily deceived in person.
57. They are more easily manipulated in person.
58. There is a study of the Watergate tapes.
59. It suggests the following.
60. People disagree more often over the phone.
61. They disagree less often in face-to-face talks.

62. These studies point to a surprising possibility.
63. They are little-known.
64. They are somewhat inconclusive.
65. The possibility is that telephones may help keep conversations more honest.

IDENTIFICATION

The nightclub comic Henny Youngman, known for years as "King of the One-Liners" because of his rapid-fire delivery of single-line jokes, became the subject of a one-liner himself in the mid-1960s. At unpredictable moments, cast members of the *Laugh-In* T.V. show would suddenly turn toward the camera with a look of dawning realization and say, "Oh . . . *that* Henny Youngman!" The complete improbability of there being any *other* Henny Youngman is what made the line funny.

While there may be only one Henny, the fact remains that there is more than one of almost everything else. Hence, we often find that we have to identify the person or thing we are talking about more specifically than is possible in a word or two. It makes no sense to say "A man stole my wallet" or "Turn left when you come to a building" if you can say "A man with a red beard stole my wallet" or "Turn left when you come to an ornate stone building." Often, as in the preceding examples, a modifier such as **ornate, stone,** or **with a red beard** can serve quite well as an identifier. (The techniques you learned in the *Description* section will help you in cases like these.) In other situations, however, a modifier won't do the trick. Look, for instance, at the following pair of sentences:

A woman had once taught school in Milwaukee.
The woman was Israel's fourth prime minister.

The second sentence certainly helps to identify the woman in the first sentence. You may notice, however, that there is no elegant way to turn the second sentence into any of the sorts of modifiers we've worked with so far. Instead, you can take advantage of a skill you learned in Part One: turning a sentence into a clause. You can, with no trouble at all, turn **The woman was Israel's fourth prime minister** into **The woman who was Israel's fourth prime minister. . . .** You can then combine that clause quite naturally with the first sentence. What you end up with is:

> The woman who was Israel's fourth prime minister once taught school in Milwaukee.

Or, if you apply this same technique the other way around, you get:

> A woman who once taught school in Milwaukee was Israel's fourth prime minister.

This section will show you how you can use techniques like this one to identify the people, places, and things that you write about. You'll also discover some new applications for the sentence combining techniques you've already learned.

Restrictive Clauses

The kind of clause used most often as an identifier is called a restrictive clause. It usually starts with **that** or **who,** but may sometimes begin with **which.** In general, a clause of this type will narrow down a general subject into something more specific. Look, for example, at the following set of sentences:

> One species of camel is called a dromedary.
> This species has one hump.

The first of these sentences clearly cries out for identification. The reader asks, "*Which* species of camel? How will I know a dromedary when I see one?" The second sentence answers the question by identifying the dromedary as the camel that has one hump. This, then, is a perfect situation in which to use a restrictive clause:

> The species of camel that has one hump is called a dromedary.

As usual, you can express the same relationship in other ways as well. The techniques you've learned in earlier sections will continue to come in handy:

One species of camel is called a dromedary; this species has one hump. [ASSOCIATION]

The species of camel with one hump is called a dromedary. [DESCRIPTION]

The one-humped species of camel is called a dromedary. [DESCRIPTION]

While the following set of exercises deals primarily with restrictive clauses, you'll discover any number of other ways to narrow a subject down from the general to the specific. Follow the models carefully, but use your imagination on line e and in the open exercises.

MODELED EXERCISE A

SIMPLE SENTENCES:
The planet Saturn has seventeen moons.
The moons orbit the planet.
They consist mainly of ice.

COMBINATIONS:
(a) The seventeen moons that orbit the planet Saturn consist mainly of ice.
(b) The planet Saturn has seventeen moons orbiting it which consist mainly of ice.
(c) Orbiting the planet Saturn are seventeen moons consisting mainly of ice.
(d) Seventeen moons consisting mainly of ice orbit the planet Saturn.

Select the combination that works best in the following context.

CONTEXT:
Although it had long been thought that they were composed of rock, it is now known that _____.

Now create similar combinations for the following sets of simple sentences. On line e, add your own combination. Then select the one that best fits the given context.

1

SIMPLE SENTENCES:
The horse has fragile legs.
The legs support the full weight of the horse.
They barely match the human wrist in thickness.

COMBINATIONS:
(a) _____
(b) _____
(c) _____
(d) _____
(e) _____

CONTEXT:
_____. This is often in excess of 900 pounds, over five times the weight of the average human being.

2

SIMPLE SENTENCES:
Ossabaw Island has an impressive forest.
The forest dominates the island.
It consists of mature live oaks and pines.

COMBINATIONS:
(a) _____
(b) _____
(c) _____
(d) _____
(e) _____

CONTEXT:
Majestically _____. Many of the trees are 200 years old or more, making the forest extremely unusual for the United States. Ossabaw Island is one of the treasures of the Georgia coastline.

3

SIMPLE SENTENCES:
Iceland has natural hot springs.
The hot springs heat Iceland's homes.
They vary in temperature.

COMBINATIONS:
(a) _____
(b) _____
(c) _____
(d) _____
(e) _____

CONTEXT:
Originating deep underground, _____. The heat is probably of volcanic origin, for Iceland has many active volcanos.

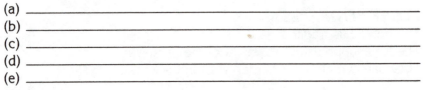

4

Complete the simple sentences by filling in the blanks. Then create a set of combinations as before.

SIMPLE SENTENCES:
_____ has many resources.
The resources strengthen _____.
They include _____.

COMBINATIONS:
(a) _____
(b) _____
(c) _____
(d) _____
(e) _____

OPEN EXERCISE A

The following simple sentences constitute a short essay called "The Duke Ellington Difference." Rewrite the sentences in essay form. (A gap between lines indicates that you should start a new paragraph.) You will notice that sentences 12–14 and 45–47 are of the type you have worked with in the previous exercise. Compare your finished essay with those of your classmates and be prepared to discuss the choices you have made.

1. Duke Ellington has a position.
2. His position is in the world of music.

3. His position there is unique.
4. He was an excellent jazz pianist.
5. He was a composer.
6. He was an arranger.
7. He was one of the best in the history of jazz.
8. He was a bandleader.
9. This fact is important.
10. Most composers do not have bands.
11. Ellington had an advantage.
12. He had a fine band.
13. The band inspired him.
14. It consisted of talented musicians.
15. His band performed his works.
16. This insured a proper interpretation of his music.
17. It shaped his compositions and arrangements.

18. The musicians in the band were individualistic.
19. They were temperamental.
20. This did not matter to Ellington.
21. He knew their talents.
22. He knew their limitations.
23. He wrote music with those things in mind.
24. This had a result.
25. The music sounded better.
26. It was suited to the musicians' talents.
27. The musicians sounded better.
28. They were suited to the music.
29. This has been noted.

30. The musicians also made a contribution.
31. They made suggestions to Ellington.
32. They suggested how something could be played.
33. They suggested how a composition could be improved.
34. Ellington listened to these suggestions.
35. He often changed compositions.
36. He gave his musicians credit.
37. He listed their names as composers of certain pieces.
38. Their names were listed along with his own.
39. This collaborative process continued throughout Ellington's career.
40. Ellington had a long career.

41. He made many tours.
42. The tours were frequent.
43. They were to all parts of the world.
44. These two things had a result.
45. He had a large, international audience.
46. The audience eagerly awaited his works.
47. It included two types of people.
48. Some were devotees of "pure jazz."
49. This audience preferred certain works.
50. These works include *Black and Tan Fantasy.*
51. They include *The C Jam Blues.*
52. There is another audience.
53. This audience is larger.
54. This audience prefers certain other compositions.
55. These compositions include *Sophisticated Lady.*
56. They include *Mood Indigo.*
57. These works are well known.
58. They are standards.
59. They have become a permanent part of popular music.

MODELED EXERCISE B

SIMPLE SENTENCES:
Captain James Cook traveled in Australia.
While traveling, he saw an animal.
It carried its young in a pouch.

COMBINATIONS:
(a) Captain James Cook, while traveling in Australia, saw an animal
    that carried its young in a pouch.
(b) An animal that Captain James Cook saw while traveling in Aus-
    tralia carried its young in a pouch.
(c) Captain James Cook traveled in Australia; he saw an animal that
    carried its young in a pouch.
(d) While he was traveling in Australia, Captain James Cook saw an
    animal that carried its young in a pouch.

Select the combination that works best in the following context.

CONTEXT:
The English explorer ———————————. He asked the aborigines what they called this strange animal. They answered "kangaroo," which in their language means "I do not know." The name has remained ever since.

Now create similar combinations for the following sets of simple sentences. On line e, add your own combination. Then select the one that best fits the given context.

1

SIMPLE SENTENCES:
Tantalus was admitted to Olympus.
After being admitted there, he stole nectar.
It belonged to the Greek gods.

COMBINATIONS:
(a) ——————————————————————————
(b) ——————————————————————————
(c) ——————————————————————————
(d) ——————————————————————————
(e) ——————————————————————————

CONTEXT:
The ambrosia and ———————————. The gods punished him by putting him in a pool in which the level of water sank out of his reach each time he bent to take a drink. Tantalus's punishment in this well-known myth gave rise to the English word **tantalize.**

2

SIMPLE SENTENCES:
Count Rumford tested the caloric theory.
While testing it, he performed an experiment.
It showed how friction could boil water.

COMBINATIONS:
(a) ——————————————————————————
(b) ——————————————————————————

(c) _____

(d) _____

(e) _____

CONTEXT:

Until the late 1700s, people thought of heat as an invisible, weightless fluid called caloric. They thought caloric flowed from a hot body into a cold body to heat the cold one. This caloric theory was tested by many scientists, one of whom was Benjamin Thompson, also called Count Rumford. _____. By boiling the water without apparent heat, he astonished many people.

3

SIMPLE SENTENCES:

Irving Janis studied the Bay of Pigs fiasco.
While studying it, he researched psychological pressures.
They lessen a group's decision-making ability.

COMBINATIONS:

(a) _____

(b) _____

(c) _____

(d) _____

(e) _____

CONTEXT:

Author _____and pave the way for errors in judgment. In his book *Victims of Groupthink* he suggests that the human drive for conformity often overrides the ability to think objectively and to disagree.

4

Complete the simple sentences by filling in the blanks. Then create a set of combinations as before.

SIMPLE SENTENCES:

_____performs services.
As it performs them, it uses many taxpayer dollars.
These _____.

COMBINATIONS:
(a) _____
(b) _____
(c) _____
(d) _____
(e) _____

OPEN EXERCISE B

The following simple sentences constitute a short essay called "Oh, What Tangled Webs." Rewrite the sentences in essay form. (A gap between lines indicates that you should start a new paragraph.) You will notice that sentences 21–23 and 31–33 are of the type you have worked with in the previous exercise. Compare your finished essay with those of your classmates and be prepared to discuss the choices you have made.

1. Spiders can secrete silk.
2. They can also spin webs.
3. These abilities are characteristics of nearly all spiders.
4. The characteristics are distinctive.
5. Each web-spinning spider has its own special pattern.
6. It is usually possible to identify a spider.
7. The type of web the spider weaves identifies it.
8. Spider silk is secreted by glands.
9. These glands are located in the lower part of the abdomen.
10. The silken strands are issued from small, nipple-like openings.
11. These openings are called spinnerets.
12. Spiders put their silk to use.
13. They make webs to capture insect prey.
14. This is perhaps the most interesting use.

15. Orb weavers are members of the spider family *Araneidae*.
16. They create one of the most artistic webs.
17. They create one of the most beautiful webs.
18. An orb weaver does this in the following way.
19. First it finds an open area.
20. Often this is near a path.
21. Then it climbs to an elevated place.

22. After doing this, it secretes a silken line.
23. The line is nearly weightless.
24. Eventually, a breeze floats the line across the open space.
25. The line floats until it attaches to an object.
26. Next, the spider goes across on the line.
27. The spider adds additional silk as it goes.
28. This line is the foundation line.
29. Other strands of silk are then spun.
30. They form a basic framework for the web.
31. The spider finishes the framework.
32. After finishing it, the spider spins strands of silk.
33. These strands form the various spokes of the web.
34. Up to this point the silken strands are not sticky.
35. Now the spider spins an adhesive thread.
36. This thread will actually entrap the prey.
37. The spider starts at the outside edge.
38. It works inward.
39. It goes around and around.
40. It adds more sticky strands as it goes.

41. The spider's web is completed.
42. The spider may return to the center of the web.
43. It may hide in a nearby retreat.
44. It awaits the capture of an insect in the sticky web.
45. The captured prey is usually bound in bands of silk.
46. This happens before the spider kills the prey.
47. The spider then sucks out the prey's body fluids.
48. The web is usually good for only one night.
49. This is interesting.
50. By dawn it is in tatters.

MODELED EXERCISE C

SIMPLE SENTENCES:
Paper may be made from wood.
It can crumble in just thirty years.
Paper may be made from cloth.
It can last hundreds of years.

COMBINATIONS:
(a) Paper that is made from wood can crumble in just thirty years, whereas paper made from cloth can last hundreds of years.
(b) Paper can crumble in just thirty years when made from wood but can last hundreds of years when made from cloth.
(c) Unlike paper made from cloth, which can last hundreds of years, paper made from wood can crumble in just thirty years.
(d) Paper that can last hundreds of years may be made from cloth, although paper made from wood can crumble in just thirty years.

Select the combination that works best in the following context.

CONTEXT:
A process to make paper out of wood was introduced in 1880. It was not until years later that a drawback of this process came to light. Angry book owners discovered that _____.

Now create similar combinations for the following sets of simple sentences. On line e, add your own combination. Then select the one that best fits the given context.

1

SIMPLE SENTENCES:
Chimpanzees can be raised in cages.
They show severe emotional disturbances.
Chimpanzees can be raised in grassy enclosures.
They form normal social bonds.

COMBINATIONS:
(a) _____
(b) _____
(c) _____
(d) _____
(e) _____

CONTEXT:
Believed by many to be man's closest relatives in the animal kingdom, _____. This reaction seems to show how crucial early experience is to the development of character.

2

SIMPLE SENTENCES:
Telescopes can be built with a single lens.
They distort the image.
Telescopes can be built with several small lenses.
They produce a clear image.

COMBINATIONS:

(a) _____
(b) _____
(c) _____
(d) _____
(e) _____

CONTEXT:
In technology, the simplest method isn't always the best. _____
_____and are therefore much easier to focus.

3

SIMPLE SENTENCES:
Data banks can be set up on magnetic tape.
They may take several minutes to yield information.
Data banks can be created on silicon chips.
They yield information almost instantly.

COMBINATIONS:

(a) _____
(b) _____
(c) _____
(d) _____
(e) _____

CONTEXT:
Auxiliary computer storage, usually on tape, is much less accessible than main computer memory. _____. However, they are preferable precisely because they do not take up space in main storage.

4

Complete the simple sentences by filling in the blanks. Then create a set of combinations as before.

SIMPLE SENTENCES:
Frankfurters can be made from beef or pork.
They _____.
Frankfurters can be made from chicken.
They _____.

COMBINATIONS:
(a) _____
(b) _____
(c) _____
(d) _____
(e) _____

OPEN EXERCISE C

The following simple sentences constitute a short essay called "Ultralight Airplanes." Rewrite the sentences in essay form. (A gap between lines indicates that you should start a new paragraph.) You will notice that sentences 1 through 4 are of the type you have worked with in the previous exercise. Compare your finished essay with those of your classmates and be prepared to discuss the choices you have made.

1. Planes can be made for transportation.
2. They tend to be very expensive.
3. Planes can be made for pleasure.
4. They can now be purchased for very little.
5. To have a certain airplane has been a dream.
6. The airplane is inexpensive.
7. Flying the airplane is not difficult.
8. The dream has been shared by many people.
9. This has been so since the earliest days of aviation.
10. The dream has come true.

11. The dream was long held.
12. This happened only within the past few years.
13. It had a cause.
14. The cause was that two principles have been combined.
15. One is the principle of the hang glider.
16. One is the principle of the small engine.
17. The combining had a result.
18. The result was to bring an airplane into being.
19. The airplane is the ultralight airplane.
20. Models are available today.
21. They are numerous.
22. They are within a price range.
23. The price range is reasonable.
24. To fly the craft is not hard.
25. This is so for a pilot with proper training.

26. Ultralight planes have been marketed.
27. They have been marketed as "air recreational vehicles."
28. They have been a success.
29. The success has been commercial.
30. The success has been great.
31. Their popularity has three main reasons.
32. This seems to be so.
33. One reason is affordability.
34. Another reason is convenience.
35. Another reason is pleasure.
36. The pleasure is sheer.
37. The pleasure is in flying in this way.
38. The pilot is not enclosed in a cockpit.
39. The pilot is exposed to the air.
40. The pilot is exposed to the wind.
41. The engine can be turned off.
42. The craft can soar.
43. The soaring is like that of a glider.
44. The airplane is convenient.
45. This is so back on the ground.
46. The airplane can be folded up.
47. The airplane can be stored.
48. The storing occurs at home.

MODELED EXERCISE D

SIMPLE SENTENCES:
Certain painters were outmoded.
They were outmoded by photography.
These painters specialized in portraits.

COMBINATIONS:
(a) Painters who specialized in portraits were outmoded by photography.
(b) Photography outmoded painters who specialized in portraits.
(c) Certain painters were outmoded by photography because they specialized in portraits.
(d) If painters specialized in portraits, they were outmoded by photography.

Select the combination that works best in the following context.

CONTEXT:
_____, but had no effect on landscape painters, who did not feel the same pressures to produce an exact likeness of their subject.

Now create similar combinations for the following sets of simple sentences. On line e, add your own combination. Then select the one that best fits the given context.

1

SIMPLE SENTENCES:
Certain animals are often missed.
They are missed by predators.
These animals blend well with their surroundings.

COMBINATIONS:
(a) _____
(b) _____

(c) _____
(d) _____
(e) _____

CONTEXT:

_____. Other animals are deliberately avoided by pred-
ators because they sport threatening colors and thus stand out from
their surroundings. Both of these devices fall into the category of
protective coloration.

2

SIMPLE SENTENCES:
Certain urban crime drives away business.
It drives it away from inner cities.
That crime threatens property.

COMBINATIONS:
(a) _____
(b) _____
(c) _____
(d) _____
(e) _____

CONTEXT:
If urban crime involves vandalism or burglary, it threatens property.
_____. If it drives business away, the whole community
suffers.

3

SIMPLE SENTENCES:
Certain French aristocrats were executed.
They were executed on the guillotine.
Those aristocrats opposed the Revolution.

COMBINATIONS:
(a) _____
(b) _____

(c) _____

(d) _____

(e) _____

CONTEXT:

As the citizens of the Republic gained power, _____,
the new "humane" instrument of death. Actually, Dr. Guillotin's machine was inhuman in its cold efficiency.

4

*Complete the simple sentence by filling in the blank. Then create a
set of combinations as before.*

SIMPLE SENTENCES:

Certain athletes succeed.

They succeed in making fortunes.

Those athletes _____.

COMBINATIONS:

(a) _____

(b) _____

(c) _____

(d) _____

(e) _____

OPEN EXERCISE D

*The following simple sentences constitute a short essay called "Com-
mercials Through the Years." Sentences 52 through 59 are missing;
you will have to supply these yourself. (The general topic of the sentences you write should be the form that product advertisements may
take in the near future. Feel free to add more or fewer than the specified
number of sentences if you think that doing so will improve the essay.)*

*Rewrite the sentences in essay form. (A gap between lines indicates
that you should start a new paragraph.) You will notice that sentences
11–13 and 21–23 are of the type you have worked with in the previous*

exercise. Some of the sentences you supply should be of this type as well.

Compare your finished essay with those of your classmates and be prepared to discuss the choices you have made.

1. Commercials have been a central feature.
2. They have been a feature of American television.
3. This has been true since its early days.
4. Commercial television has existed for more than three decades.
5. T.V. ads have changed during this time.
6. They have gone through a complex evolution.

7. There was a first stage.
8. Commercials spoke for the seller.
9. They displayed certain product features.
10. These features were important to the advertiser.
11. Live demonstrations were conducted.
12. They were conducted by cheerful announcers.
13. These demonstrations stressed the product's selling points.
14. The demonstrations sometimes backfired.
15. This greatly delighted viewers.

16. There was a second stage.
17. Advertising agencies took control.
18. Television programs were growing more sophisticated.
19. This was happening in the late 1960s.
20. Commercials had to compete with them.
21. Certain commercials were noticed.
22. They were noticed by viewers.
23. These commercials used imaginative sales techniques.
24. This was a phase of advertising.
25. The phase was creative.
26. It made use of humor.
27. It made use of bizarre visual effects.
28. These things entertained the T.V. audience.

29. Such commercials were clever.
30. They pleased viewers.
31. They didn't always increase sales.

32. This had a result.
33. Commercials began to change again.
34. There was a third stage.
35. It used psychological techniques.
36. The techniques were to convince viewers to buy the product.
37. Commercials would sometimes repeat a message endlessly.
38. They would succeed in invading a viewer's awareness.
39. This was simply because they were so annoying.
40. Sometimes they would use a different technique.
41. They would send a message.
42. The message would be very subtle.
43. The viewer would not even notice the message consciously.
44. But the viewer would respond.

45. Network television today is running into competition.
46. The competition is from new media.
47. Among these new media is cable T.V.
48. Among these new media are video games.
49. Among these new media are video recorders.
50. Product advertising will no doubt change again.
51. It may take a whole new form.
52. _____
53. _____
54. _____
55. _____
56. _____
57. _____
58. _____
59. _____
60. We can be sure of one thing.
61. Commercials will not vanish from American life.
62. This will be true no matter what happens.

Nonrestrictive Clauses

As you've seen, a restrictive clause always works as an identifier—it narrows down its subject into something more specific. There is another type of clause, however, that does not always work this way. A *nonrestrictive clause* simply comments on the subject of the sentence;

it does not necessarily narrow it down. The following sentences will serve as an example:

Potatoes are actually enlarged stems.
The French call them "apples of the earth."

When we combine these sentences using a nonrestrictive clause, we get:

Potatoes, which the French call "apples of the earth," are actually enlarged stems.

Note that the clause **which the French call "apples of the earth"** does nothing to make **potatoes** more specific; the French call *all* potatoes "apples of the earth," and *all* potatoes are enlarged stems. **Potatoes** remains a relatively general word in the sentence.

On the other hand, a nonrestrictive clause *can* help to identify a subject—just as a modifier can. Look, for instance, at the following simple sentences:

Burmese merchants measure rice in tengs.
Tengs are units of volume.

These can be combined to form:

Burmese merchants measure rice in tengs, which are units of volume.

Once again, the clause **which are units of volume** does nothing to narrow down **tengs,** since *all* tengs are units of volume. On the other hand, if you didn't know what tengs are (and we'll bet you didn't!), the nonrestrictive clause certainly identified them for you.

Remember that, as usual, you can use other sorts of combinations besides nonrestrictive clauses to express the same relationships. Let's return from rice to potatoes to demonstrate some of the possibilities:

Potatoes are actually enlarged stems, but the French call them "apples of the earth." [ASSOCIATION]

Potatoes are actually enlarged stems; the French call them "apples of the earth." [ASSOCIATION]

Called "apples of the earth" by the French, potatoes are actually enlarged stems. [DESCRIPTION]

Actually, the enlarged stems that the French call "apples of the earth" are potatoes. [IDENTIFICATION]

There are other possible combinations, of course; you'll discover some of them as you work on this next set of exercises.

MODELED EXERCISE A

SIMPLE SENTENCES:
Abraham Lincoln moved to the Indiana frontier at age seven.
He was born in Kentucky.

COMBINATIONS:
(a) Abraham Lincoln, who moved to the Indiana frontier at age seven, was born in Kentucky.
(b) Abraham Lincoln, who was born in Kentucky, moved to the Indiana frontier at age seven.
(c) Abraham Lincoln was born in Kentucky and moved to the Indiana frontier at age seven.
(d) Abraham Lincoln moved to the Indiana frontier at age seven; he was born in Kentucky.

Select the combination that works best in the following context.

CONTEXT:
Usually associated with Illinois, _____. It wasn't until he was twenty-one that his family finally settled in Decatur, Illinois.

Now create similar combinations for the following sets of simple sentences. On line e, add your own combination. Then select the one that best fits the given context.

1

SIMPLE SENTENCES:
Game theory deals with conflict and choice.
It is a branch of mathematics.

COMBINATIONS:
(a) _____
(b) _____
(c) _____
(d) _____
(e) _____

CONTEXT:
Based on the work of an American mathematician, John Von Neumann, _____used in military and business decision-making.

2

SIMPLE SENTENCES:
Domestic rabbits are descended from the European rabbit.
They were brought to this country by immigrants.

COMBINATIONS:
(a) _____
(b) _____
(c) _____
(d) _____
(e) _____

CONTEXT:
The animals we call "rabbits" actually fall into two distinct groups.
Wild rabbits, many of which are technically hares, are native to the
United States; _____from central and southern Europe.

3

SIMPLE SENTENCES:
Kindergarteners should concentrate on social skills.
They are part of a large peer group for perhaps the first time.

COMBINATIONS:

(a) _____

(b) _____

(c) _____

(d) _____

(e) _____

CONTEXT:

Some educators feel that the kindergarten classroom puts too much pressure on its pupils. They argue that _____and should probably not be burdened with academic pressure.

<h2 style="text-align:center">4</h2>

Complete the simple sentences by filling in the blanks. Then create a set of combinations as before.

SIMPLE SENTENCES:

Music clearly affects our _____.

It is often _____.

COMBINATIONS:

(a) _____

(b) _____

(c) _____

(d) _____

(e) _____

OPEN EXERCISE A

The following simple sentences constitute a short essay called "The Great Waves." Rewrite the sentences in essay form. (A gap between lines indicates that you should start a new paragraph.) You will notice that sentences 17–18 and 24–25 are of the type you have worked with in the previous exercise. Compare your finished essay with those of your classmates and be prepared to discuss the choices you have made.

1. Ocean waves have a cause.

2. The cause is usually wind.
3. A wind may ripple the surface of a lake.
4. You may have seen this happen.
5. Other winds have the same effect.
6. These winds blow over the ocean.
7. The winds may get stronger.
8. They may continue to blow from the same direction.
9. This will have a result.
10. The result is that the ripples grow into waves.
11. The winds may get stronger still.
12. They may get steadier.
13. As this happens, the waves get bigger.

14. There are other waves, however.
15. Wind does not cause them.
16. Tidal waves are one example.
17. These waves have nothing to do with tides.
18. They are taller than most buildings.
19. They are caused by earthquakes.
20. The earthquakes happen on the ocean floor.
21. The sea floor heaves and buckles.
22. It pushes upward.
23. The water above it becomes a long wave.
24. This wave may be only a few feet high at first.
25. It moves across the ocean.
26. It grows rapidly as it travels.
27. It can move at hundreds of miles an hour.
28. It may grow to be nearly 100 feet high.
29. It finally reaches land.
30. There it can cause widespread flooding.
31. There it can cause widespread destruction.

32. You might be on shore as a tidal wave approached.
33. You would first notice a drop in the sea level.
34. It would seem as if the tide were low.
35. The lowness would be unusual.
36. After a few minutes you would see a rise.
37. The rise would be rapid.
38. It would be far higher than the highest tide.
39. You would see it as the wave itself moved in.

40. The wave would be giant.

41. Tidal waves enjoy a reputation.
42. Their reputation is worldwide.
43. Scientists everywhere call them tsunamis.
44. That is their name in Japanese.

MODELED EXERCISE B

SIMPLE SENTENCES:
Iodine prevents simple goiter.
It is found in most seafoods.
This is fortunate.

COMBINATIONS:
(a) Iodine, which prevents simple goiter, is fortunately found in most seafoods.
(b) Fortunately found in most seafoods, iodine prevents simple goiter.
(c) Iodine prevents simple goiter; it is fortunately found in most seafoods.
(d) Iodine, which is fortunately found in most seafoods, prevents simple goiter.

Select the combination that works best in the following context.

CONTEXT:
The trace element _____. This is an unsightly swelling on the neck that may cause breathing difficulty as it presses on the windpipe.

Now create similar combinations for the following sets of simple sentences. On line e, add your own combination. Then select the one that best fits the given context.

1

SIMPLE SENTENCES:
Wage and price controls can curb inflation.
They were used by President Nixon.
This was successful.

COMBINATIONS:

(a) _____

(b) _____

(c) _____

(d) _____

(e) _____

CONTEXT:

Although they were _____only temporarily. If the controls are lifted, prices invariably soar again; if they remain in place, they can cause severe long-term damage to the economy.

2

SIMPLE SENTENCES:

American literature had imitated European models.

It was now developing a voice of its own.

This development was confident.

COMBINATIONS:

(a) _____

(b) _____

(c) _____

(d) _____

(e) _____

CONTEXT:

Until the nineteenth century, _____in the work of such writers as Walt Whitman and Edgar Allan Poe.

3

SIMPLE SENTENCES:

Great Britain reached its current position 10,000 years ago.

It is sinking into the North Sea.

The sinking is gradual.

COMBINATIONS:

(a) _____

(b) _____

(c) _____

(d) _____

(e) _____

CONTEXT:

The theory of plate tectonics tells us that the world's land masses are constantly in motion. Nothing lasts forever; even the seemingly immortal island of _____.

4

Complete the simple sentences by filling in the blanks. Then create a set of combinations as before.

SIMPLE SENTENCES:

Designer clothes cost extra money.

They are _____.

This is _____.

COMBINATIONS:

(a) _____

(b) _____

(c) _____

(d) _____

(e) _____

OPEN EXERCISE B

The following simple sentences constitute a short essay called "The Acropolis: A Survivor." Rewrite the sentences in essay form. (A gap between lines indicates that you should start a new paragraph.) You will notice that sentences 11–13 and 32–34 are of the type you have worked with in the previous exercise. Compare your finished essay with those of your classmates and be prepared to discuss the choices you have made.

1. The Acropolis is a hill.
2. It rises high above a city.
3. That city is Athens.

4.   The Acropolis was sacred to the ancient Greeks.
5.   It is crowned with temples.
6.   The temples are many.
7.   The temples are marble.
8.   The main temple is the Parthenon.
9.   It is dedicated to a goddess.
10. The goddess is Athena Parthenos.
11. The building is a long rectangle.
12. It is surrounded with tall columns.
13. This is impressive.
14. The Acropolis's buildings are classical.
15. They were built in the fifth century B.C.
16. They were designed by an architect.
17. His name was Phidias.
18. Athens had many craftsmen.
19. Almost all were enlisted.
20. They worked on the project.
21. It only took 15 years to complete.
22. The buildings have survived for centuries.

23. Invaders have come since then.
24. They have come in waves.
25. They were Persians.
26. They were Romans.
27. They were Crusaders.
28. They were Turks.
29. They tore down the buildings.
30. They defaced the buildings.
31. They remodeled the buildings.
32. Lord Elgin was a nineteenth century Scottish aristocrat.
33. He removed major pieces of sculpture.
34. This was bold.
35. Earthquakes have damaged the structures.
36. Air pollution has damaged the structures.
37. This has happened more recently.
38. The air pollution is severe.

39. The Acropolis's temples are now ruins.
40. The ruins gape.
41. Their marble was once painted.

42. It was painted in bright colors.
43. The marble has now weathered.
44. It is a pale golden color.
45. The Parthenon's roof is gone.
46. The hill itself is crumbling at the edges.
47. Work is going on today.
48. It is major restoration work.
49. It will preserve the Acropolis.
50. It will protect the Acropolis.
51. Then it will stand for centuries more.
52. It will stand as a monument to classical Greece.
53. It will also stand as a record.
54. It has lived through centuries.
55. The record will be of those centuries.

MODELED EXERCISE C

SIMPLE SENTENCES:
The dinosaurs lived on land.
No larger animals ever lived on land.
They died out 63 million years ago.

COMBINATIONS:
(a) No larger animals than the dinosaurs, which died out 63 million years ago, ever lived on land.
(b) The largest animals ever to live on land, the dinosaurs, died out 63 million years ago.
(c) Sixty-three million years ago, the dinosaurs, the largest animals ever to live on land, died out.
(d) The dinosaurs died out 63 million years ago; no larger animals ever lived on land.

Select the combination that works best in the following context.

CONTEXT:
For reasons still not understood by science, _____, but their power and bulk were no defense against rapid extinction.

Now create similar combinations for the following sets of simple sentences. On line e, add your own combination. Then select the one that best fits the given context.

1

SIMPLE SENTENCES:
Henry Aaron played the game of baseball.
No more consistent home-run hitter ever played the game of baseball.
Henry Aaron hit over 700 home runs in his career.

COMBINATIONS:
(a) _____
(b) _____
(c) _____
(d) _____
(e) _____

CONTEXT:
Without a doubt, _____. However, his best in any one season was 44 home runs—a long way behind Babe Ruth's epoch-making 60.

2

SIMPLE SENTENCES:
Supertankers sail the seas.
No larger vessels have ever sailed the seas.
Supertankers have to unload at offshore facilities in most places.

COMBINATIONS:
(a) _____
(b) _____
(c) _____
(d) _____
(e) _____

CONTEXT:
A few seaports can accommodate vessels of all sizes. But _____ _____. An undersea pipeline usually carries the oil ashore.

3

SIMPLE SENTENCES:
D.W. Griffith used sophisticated techniques.
No earlier filmmaker used such sophisticated techniques.
He directed several important feature-length films in the silent era.

COMBINATIONS:
(a) _____
(b) _____
(c) _____
(d) _____
(e) _____

CONTEXT:
Nowadays, when we go to the movies, we take it for granted that the camera will change positions as it records the action. There will be long shots, close-ups, and tracking shots. However, these devices had to be invented. _____, His most famous is *Birth of a Nation* (1915).

4

Complete the simple sentences by filling in the blanks. Then create a set of combinations as before.

SIMPLE SENTENCES:
_____teaches this course.
No more _____instructor has ever taught this course.
[S]he _____in class.

COMBINATIONS:
(a) _____
(b) _____
(c) _____
(d) _____
(e) _____

OPEN EXERCISE C

The following simple sentences constitute a short essay called "Glass-making: An Ancient Art." Rewrite the sentences in essay form. (A gap between lines indicates that you should start a new paragraph.) You will notice that sentences 1–3 and 25–27 are of the type you have worked with in the previous exercise. Compare your finished essay with those of your classmates and be prepared to discuss the choices you have made.

1. Some ancient beads and amulets have been found.
2. No earlier glass objects have been found.
3. They were made in Mesopotamia over 3500 years ago.
4. The Mesopotamians had a way to make glass.
5. It was very simple.
6. They began with silica.
7. Silica can be found in sand.
8. It can be found in other materials.
9. The Mesopotamians probably used sand.
10. Sand was plentiful and cheap.
11. They added alkali.
12. The alkali was in a form.
13. The form was probably wood ash or plant ash.
14. It was added for a reason.
15. Alkali lowers the melting temperature of sand.
16. They added lime.
17. The lime was from crushed stone.
18. They heated the ingredients together.
19. This had a result.
20. The ingredients turned to glass.
21. This is the basic recipe.
22. It is still used today.

23. There was a later innovation.
24. It came about in Roman times.
25. Glassblowing was developed.
26. No more important technique has been developed in the history of glassmaking.
27. Glassblowing came into practice around 100 B.C.
28. Glassblowing works in the following way.
29. When glass is heated, it becomes liquid.
30. It pours.
31. It becomes pliable as it cools.
32. It does not become rigid until it has cooled completely.
33. Until then, it can be rolled.
34. It can be molded.
35. It can be blown.

36. Glassblowing is like blowing a soap bubble.
37. There is a difference.
38. A glass blower can control the shape of the bubble.
39. Glassblowing is still done today.
40. It is done differently.
41. Machines are used.
42. They can blow glass.
43. These machines were invented in the nineteenth century.
44. They are widely used.
45. They make industrial products.
46. An example is lightbulbs.
47. They are made on glassblowing machines.
48. Now there are other machines as well.
49. An example is machines that roll glass.
50. Plate glass is made on these machines.

51. There are still artisans.
52. They blow glass.
53. They use the old methods.
54. The objects they make are beautiful.
55. The objects they make are expensive.
56. The objects they make are much in demand.
57. Glassmaking is still an art form.
58. This is so when it is in these artisans' hands.

MODELED EXERCISE D

SIMPLE SENTENCES:
Jet planes can be made from plastic.
Jet planes can be made from aluminum.
Plastic is lighter than aluminum.
Light planes have an advantage.
They use less fuel.

COMBINATIONS:
(a) Plastic jet planes, which are lighter than aluminum jet planes, have the advantage of using less fuel.
(b) Jet planes made from plastic are lighter than those made from aluminum and thus have the advantage of using less fuel.

(c) Jet planes of plastic, because they are lighter than jet planes of aluminum, have the advantage of using less fuel.
(d) The advantage of plastic jet planes over aluminum jet planes is that they are lighter and use less fuel.

Select the combination that works best in the following context.

CONTEXT:
Plastic is generally thought of as a material used to save money. But _____, not that they are less expensive to build.

Now create similar combinations for the following sets of simple sentences. On line e, add your own combination. Then select the one that best fits the given context.

1

SIMPLE SENTENCES:
Submarine hulls can be made from glass.
Submarine hulls can be made from steel.
Glass is more pressure-resistant than steel.
Pressure-resistant hulls have an advantage.
They are capable of reaching greater depths.

COMBINATIONS:
(a) _____
(b) _____
(c) _____
(d) _____
(e) _____

CONTEXT:
Although glass is, for all practical purposes, a solid, its molecular structure is that of a liquid. This unique property makes glass particularly useful in high-pressure environments. In the ocean, for instance,

2

SIMPLE SENTENCES:
Tennis rackets can be made of graphite.
Tennis rackets can be made of wood.
Graphite is stiffer than wood.
Stiff rackets have an advantage.
They produce more power.

COMBINATIONS:
(a) _____
(b) _____
(c) _____
(d) _____
(e) _____

CONTEXT:
_____. However, wood tennis rackets, which are more flexible, can be more easily controlled by the amateur.

3

SIMPLE SENTENCES:
Hedges can be made up of deciduous shrubs.
Hedges can be made up of evergreens.
Deciduous shrubs are faster-growing than evergreens.
Fast-growing hedges have an advantage.
They make a screen sooner.

COMBINATIONS:
(a) _____
(b) _____
(c) _____
(d) _____
(e) _____

CONTEXT:
_____. On the other hand, hedges of evergreens, because they never shed all of their needles at once, have the advantage of making a screen even in the winter.

4

Complete the simple sentences by filling in the blanks. Then create a set of combinations as before.

SIMPLE SENTENCES:
Food wrapping can be plastic.
Food wrapping can be paper.
Plastic is _____than paper.
_____wrapping has an advantage.
It _____.

COMBINATIONS:
(a) _____
(b) _____
(c) _____
(d) _____
(e) _____

OPEN EXERCISE D

The following simple sentences constitute a short essay called "Breaking the Habit." Sentences 5 through 10 are missing; you will have to supply these yourself. (The general topic of the sentences you write should be the unhealthy effects that smoking and overeating have on the body. Feel free to add more or fewer than the specified number of sentences if you think that doing so will improve the essay.)

Rewrite the sentences in essay form. (A gap between lines indicates that you should start a new paragraph.) You will notice that sentences 47 through 51 are of the type you have worked with in the previous exercise. Some of the sentences you supply should be of this type as well.

Compare your finished essay with those of your classmates and be prepared to discuss the choices you have made.

1. Smoking is a dangerous habit.
2. Overeating is a dangerous habit.

3. Most people are aware of this by now.
4. Their effects on the body are well known.
5. _____
6. _____
7. _____
8. _____
9. _____
10. _____
11. However, something else is generally accepted.
12. It is that smoking is a difficult condition to correct.
13. It is that overeating is a difficult condition to correct.
14. A psychiatrist drew a conclusion.
15. The psychiatrist had examined case studies.
16. The studies were numerous.
17. The studies involved obesity.
18. The conclusion was depressing.
19. Many people seek treatment for obesity.
20. The conclusion was that most do so in vain.
21. People have reviewed other literature.
22. The literature is on cigarette smoking.
23. Those people are similarly pessimistic.

24. Smoking is a behavior.
25. Overeating is a behavior.
26. Professionals share a belief.
27. It is that these behaviors are nearly impossible to change.
28. There are grounds for questioning this belief.
29. Millions of Americans have dropped one or both habits.
30. They have succeeded in doing so.
31. Surveys show this.
32. People have quit smoking.
33. People have shed pounds.
34. The shedding is permanent.
35. Virtually everyone knows such people personally.

36. There is a discrepancy between opinion and fact.
37. The opinion is professional.
38. The fact is apparent.
39. There is an explanation for this discrepancy.
40. The explanation may be quite simple.

41.   Two points have generally been overlooked.
42.   The points are important.
43.   One point is as follows.
44.   The case studies are only about certain people.
45.   These people went to a therapist for help.
46.   The other point is as follows.
47.   Opinions can be based on surveys.
48.   Opinions can be based on case studies.
49.   Surveys include more people than case studies.
50.   Opinions based on more people have an advantage.
51.   They are more likely to be sound.
52.   We may take these points into account.
53.   Doing so makes the following idea easier to believe.
54.   Smoking and overeating are habits.
55.   The habits are health-endangering.
56.   People have difficulty in breaking these habits.
57.   The difficulty has been exaggerated.
58.   The exaggeration has been great.

Appositives

The nonrestrictive clauses that most directly identify their subjects are those that include simple forms of the verb **to be**—words such as **is, was, are,** and **were.** These verbs occur in each of the following pairs of sentences:

Belize was once known as British Honduras.
It is a tiny Central American country.

Mozart composed music for the glass harmonica.
The glass harmonica is a series of glass discs played with moistened fingers.

Sobhuza died in 1982.
He was king of Swaziland for more than 80 years.

If we combine these sentences using a nonrestrictive clause, we get:

Belize, which is a tiny Central American country, was once known as British Honduras.

Mozart composed music for the glass harmonica, which is a series of glass discs played with moistened fingers.

Sobhuza, who was king of Swaziland for more than 80 years, died in 1982.

Although these combinations are all grammatically correct, you've probably noticed that they sound quite awkward. Fortunately, the English language provides us with an elegant device for rescuing sentences like these. By removing the pronoun (**who** or **which**) and the verb (some form of **to be**), we can change the identifying clause to an identifying *phrase* and thus make the sentence flow much more smoothly. The phrase that results is called an ***appositive,*** and, when used in our sample sentences, it looks like this:

Belize, a tiny Central American country, was once known as British Honduras.

Mozart composed music for the glass harmonica, a series of glass discs played with moistened fingers.

Sobhuza, king of Swaziland for more than 80 years, died in 1982.

The appositive, as you'll discover in the following exercises, is quite a useful device for identification. Since it is so closely related to the nonrestrictive clause—which you've already worked with extensively— we've included fewer exercises than we have in other sections.

MODELED EXERCISE A

SIMPLE SENTENCES:
Adam Smith described the division of labor.
It is an economic principle.
It is classic.
It is the theory behind assembly lines.

COMBINATIONS:
(a) Adam Smith described the division of labor, a classic economic principle which is the theory behind assembly lines.
(b) The division of labor, a classic economic principle described by Adam Smith, is the theory behind assembly lines.

(c) The division of labor, a classic economic principle which is the theory behind assembly lines, was described by Adam Smith.
(d) The theory behind assembly lines is the division of labor, a classic economic principle described by Adam Smith.

Select the combination that works best in the following context.

CONTEXT:
In 1776, _____in *The Wealth of Nations.* Although Smith considered himself a philosopher, his remarkable book earned him the title "Father of Modern Economics."

Now create similar combinations for the following sets of simple sentences. On line e, add your own combination. Then select the one that best fits the given context.

1

SIMPLE SENTENCES:
Many people use acetaminophen.
It is a pain killer.
It is mild.
It is a substitute for aspirin.

COMBINATIONS:
(a) _____
(b) _____
(c) _____
(d) _____
(e) _____

CONTEXT:
_____that is frequently recommended for young children. Although it is more expensive than aspirin, it does not have some of aspirin's less desirable side effects.

2

SIMPLE SENTENCES:
Kenobi selects Han Solo.
Solo is a pilot.
He is self-assertive.
He is a key character in the plot.

COMBINATIONS:

(a) _____

(b) _____

(c) _____

(d) _____

(e) _____

CONTEXT:

A common theme in American fantasy is the self-reliant, aggressive, and ultimately warm-hearted hustler—witness the movie *Star Wars,* where _____to help defeat the Empire.

3

SIMPLE SENTENCES:

Many have idolized Calvin Coolidge.

He was a Republican.

He was pro-business.

He was successor to President Harding.

COMBINATIONS:

(a) _____

(b) _____

(c) _____

(d) _____

(e) _____

CONTEXT:

Called "silent Cal" during his vice presidency, _____.
One reason for this attitude is his reputation for honest integrity, which doubtless helped to keep his party together after Harding's so-called "Teapot Dome" scandal.

4

Complete the simple sentences by filling in the blanks. Then create a set of combinations as before.

SIMPLE SENTENCES:

Many women support feminism.

It is a political movement.

It is _____.

It is the reason for _____.

COMBINATIONS:

(a) _____

(b) _____

(c) _____

(d) _____

(e) _____

OPEN EXERCISE A

The following simple sentences constitute a short essay called "Science Fiction's Two Attitudes." Rewrite the sentences in essay form. (A gap between lines indicates that you should start a new paragraph.) You will notice that sentences 18 through 21 are of the type you have worked with in the previous exercise. Compare your finished essay with those of your classmates and be prepared to discuss the choices you have made.

1. Jules Verne was a father of science fiction.
2. H.G. Wells was a father of science fiction.
3. They held attitudes towards the future.
4. Their attitudes were different.
5. Verne was fascinated by new technology.
6. He was fascinated by what technology could achieve.
7. Wells was not terribly interested in a process.
8. That process was how machines worked.
9. Wells wanted his readers to think about a different subject.
10. The subject was the effects of scientific progress.
11. The effects were broader.
12. Verne saw the future as a land of great adventure.
13. Wells saw the future as a possible nightmare.
14. This was a split in attitudes.
15. This split has divided science fiction.
16. The split has lasted ever since Verne and Wells.

17. Here is an example.
18. Most readers are familiar with robots.
19. They are characters in science fiction.
20. They are common.
21. They are clues to a writer's attitude.

22. This is often so.
23. Robots can be servants.
24. They are efficient.
25. They serve the human race.
26. This is true for some writers.
27. Robots can be monsters.
28. They are made of metal.
29. They may go berserk.
30. This may happen at any moment.
31. This is true for other writers.
32. There are still other writers.
33. Isaac Asimov is one of them.
34. These writers look at the world from a certain perspective.
35. This perspective is through the eyes of the robot.
36. The robot is a half-human creature.
37. Sometimes it feels good to be almost human.
38. Sometimes it feels horrible.

39. Science fiction often deals with travel.
40. This travel is to other planets.
41. There are different ideas about a subject.
42. That subject is what the universe has to offer.
43. Earthlings may be trapped in the loneliness of space.
44. Earthlings may meet other races.
45. There can be contact with other civilizations.
46. This contact is in outer space.
47. This contact could be beneficial.
48. It could be dangerous.
49. It could be humiliating.
50. Some planets are foreign.
51. These planets can be paradises.
52. These paradises are lush.
53. These planets can be deserts.
54. These deserts are barren.

55. Our science is catching up now.
56. It is catching up with science fiction.
57. Some writers had the right idea.
58. This idea was about the future.
59. Which ones had it?

MODELED EXERCISE B

SIMPLE SENTENCES:
The St. Lawrence Seaway is a major waterway.
It was built by the United States and Canada.
It is navigated by many cargo ships.

COMBINATIONS:
(a) The St. Lawrence Seaway, a major waterway navigated by many cargo ships, was built by the United States and Canada.
(b) The St. Lawrence Seaway, a major waterway built by the United States and Canada, is navigated by many cargo ships.
(c) The United States and Canada built a major waterway navigated by many cargo ships—the St. Lawrence Seaway.
(d) Many cargo ships navigate the St. Lawrence Seaway, a major waterway which was built by the United States and Canada.

Select the combination that works best in the following context.

CONTEXT:
_____, which opened in 1959. Such cooperation on an international scale is rare.

Now create similar combinations for the following sets of simple sentences. On line e, add your own combination. Then select the one that best fits the given context.

1

SIMPLE SENTENCES:
"Casey at the Bat" is a famous comic poem.
It was first printed by the *San Francisco Examiner*.
It was written by Ernest Thayer.

COMBINATIONS:
(a) _____
(b) _____

(c) _____
(d) _____
(e) _____

CONTEXT:

It used to be common for poems to get their first airing in the popular press. _____. It is renowned for its last line: "But there is no joy in Mudville—mighty Casey has struck out."

2

SIMPLE SENTENCES:

The Medal of Honor is an award for bravery.
It is presented by the President.
It is received by few people.

COMBINATIONS:

(a) _____
(b) _____
(c) _____
(d) _____
(e) _____

CONTEXT:

_____. But those who do are receiving high acclaim indeed, for it is the highest military award for bravery in the United States.

3

SIMPLE SENTENCES:

King Tutankhamen's tomb was a hidden chamber.
It was finally discovered by Howard Carter.
It was preserved by fallen rocks.

COMBINATIONS:

(a) _____
(b) _____

(c) _____

(d) _____

(e) _____

CONTEXT:

We owe the greatest treasure ever recovered from the ancient world to its owner's insignificance. _____that were thrown down over the entrance. A more important tomb was being prepared higher up—and, needless to say, *that* tomb was robbed of its treasures long ago.

4

Complete the simple sentences by filling in the blanks. Then create a set of combinations as before.

SIMPLE SENTENCES:

_____was a _____.

It was mocked by _____.

It was finally recognized as a masterpiece by _____.

COMBINATIONS:

(a) _____

(b) _____

(c) _____

(d) _____

(e) _____

OPEN EXERCISE B

The following simple sentences constitute a short essay called "Background to the Witch Trials." Sentences 51 through 58 are missing; you will have to supply these yourself. (The general topic of the sentences you write should be why people in modern times do not believe in witches. Feel free to add more or fewer than the specified number of sentences if you think that doing so will improve the essay.)

Rewrite the sentences in essay form. (A gap between lines indicates that you should start a new paragraph.) You will notice that sentences

5–7 and 41–43 are of the type you have worked with in the previous exercise. Some of the sentences you supply should be of this type as well.

Compare your finished essay with those of your classmates and be prepared to discuss the choices you have made.

1. It was January 1692.
2. It was a bleak month.
3. The people were anxious.
4. They lived in the Massachusetts Bay Colony.
5. Their charter was an important document.
6. It was the basis of their laws.
7. It had been revoked by England.
8. They had an ambassador.
9. He was the Reverend Increase Mather.
10. He was in England.
11. He was negotiating a new charter.
12. Word had come back.
13. He was having little success.
14. The old charter had spelled out rights.
15. The rights were of property.
16. Now people were uncertain.
17. Where did those rights now stand?
18. People wanted to lessen their uncertainty.
19. They wanted to direct their religious vigor.
20. They wanted to further God's kingdom.
21. People needed a way to do these things.
22. The witchcraft trials are famous.
23. They started at this time.

24. There is a fact.
25. It must be considered.
26. It helps explain the general atmosphere of the time.
27. No one doubted the existence of the devil.
28. No one doubted the existence of witches.
29. These were real.
30. They could wreak havoc.
31. They had to be sought out.

32. They had to be punished.
33. Thousands had been put to death.
34. Their crime was witchcraft.
35. Most were in Europe.
36. This was in the Middle Ages.
37. A few were in the Bay Colony.
38. This was more recent.
39. One of them was a washerwoman.
40. She was called Witch Glover.
41. *Memorable Providences Relating to Witchcraft* was a book.
42. It was written by Cotton Mather.
43. It was circulated by the people.
44. It gave an account of her trial.
45. It was detailed.
46. It set the tone for the Salem Witch Trials.

47. Today things are different.
48. Most people do not believe in witches.
49. They have very good reasons.
50. The following are some of them.
51. _____
52. _____
53. _____
54. _____
55. _____
56. _____
57. _____
58. _____
59. The early settlers would not have agreed.

60. Many people were accused of witchcraft.
61. The accusations were during that year.
62. Some refused to confess.
63. They were hanged for their crime.
64. Many others confessed.
65. Their confessions implicated others.
66. This led to a chain reaction.
67. The chain reaction finally ended.
68. Twenty people had been put to death.

CAUSALITY

Most of us look skeptically upon anyone who claims to be able to predict the future. Self-proclaimed psychics, prophets, and fortune-tellers aside, people generally believe that no human being can possibly know what is going to happen next. Predicting the future is simply a fantasy, like turning lead into gold.

In practice, however, exactly the opposite is true. *All* of us predict the future, and we do it constantly. When we throw a ball, we predict—correctly—that it will land. When we pick up a book, we predict—again correctly—that it will *remain* a book and will not turn into, say, a bowl of oatmeal. We take these things for granted, but they need not necessarily be this way. It is possible to imagine, for instance, a world in which books that are picked up *always* turn into oatmeal. In that world, people would no doubt find nothing strange about going to the library for breakfast.

Fortunately, our lives are governed by one simple, easily understood rule: everything has a cause. If a ball lands, then it must have been thrown (or dropped). If a book turns into oatmeal, then somebody must have done something to *turn* it into oatmeal. Nothing happens by itself.

The other side of this rule is that every cause has an effect. (We'll leave the examples to you.) This basic principle of cause and effect is such an integral part of our thinking that we are seldom aware of using it. It should not be surprising, therefore, that our language takes some radical shortcuts when it deals with causes and effects. Take the following sentence, for example:

Nerve gas is deadly if inhaled.

This looks very much like the simple sentences we have been using throughout this book. It is far from simple, however. This one short sentence includes a cause, an effect, and a summary of the relationship between the two. If we express these ideas as simple sentences, we come up with the following:

Nerve gas may be inhaled. [CAUSE]

This will have an effect. [RELATIONSHIP]
The person who inhales it will die. [EFFECT]

These sentences can be combined in a number of ways, all of which have the same meaning as **Nerve gas is deadly if inhaled.** Among the possibilities are:

If nerve gas is inhaled, it will result in death.
The effect of inhaling nerve gas is death.
Nerve gas causes death when it is inhaled.
A person who inhales nerve gas will die.

No matter what form these sentences take, they all "predict the future"—that is, they all tell us what will happen in the future to someone who is unlucky enough to inhale nerve gas in the present. Of course, cause and effect are not restricted to the future. We often run into situations where we want to describe the cause of something that occurred in the past or is happening now. The simple sentences, in cases like these, look very much the same as before:

Hand cranks on early automobiles turned to the right. [CAUSE]
This had a result. [RELATIONSHIP]
Today's car engines all turn clockwise. [EFFECT]

The same idea might be expressed by a slightly different set of simple sentences:

Today's car engines all turn clockwise. [EFFECT]
This has a cause. [RELATIONSHIP]
Hand cranks on early automobiles turned to the right. [CAUSE]

Whichever set of simple sentences we start with, we arrive at combinations like these:

Because hand cranks on early automobiles turned to the right, today's car engines all turn clockwise.

The reason today's car engines all turn clockwise is that hand cranks on early automobiles turned to the right.

Hand cranks on early automobiles turned to the right, with the result that today's car engines all turn clockwise.

Since hand cranks on early automobiles turned to the right, today's car engines all turn clockwise.

As you can see, causes and effects that take place in the future produce combinations that look quite different than those produced by causes and effects in the past. If we call the first type of combinations **predictions,** the second type might be called **explanations.** Predictions, in their final form, often contain the words **if** (or **when**) and **then;** explanations often contain the words **because** or **since.** Both types, however, result from very similar sets of simple sentences.

As a general rule, any set of simple sentences that uses the key words **cause, result, effect,** or **reason** is probably expressing a cause-and-effect relationship. Look for ways to turn the sentences into a prediction or an explanation, and keep in mind that some of those key words will probably drop out when you combine the sentences. As long as English allows you to say **If I pick up a book, it will not turn into oatmeal,** you might as well take advantage. The following exercises will give you an opportunity to work with both kinds of causality.

MODELED EXERCISE A

SIMPLE SENTENCES:
Cortés met no resistance from the Aztecs.
This had a cause.
He was mistaken for a god.

COMBINATIONS:
(a) Since he was mistaken for a god, Cortés met no resistance from the Aztecs.
(b) Cortés met no resistance from the Aztecs because he was mistaken for a god.
(c) Cortés was mistaken for a god; therefore he met no resistance from the Aztecs.
(d) The reason Cortés met no resistance from the Aztecs was that he was mistaken for a god.

Select the combination that works best in the following context.

CONTEXT:
On first arriving in Mexico, _____. The Aztecs were impressed by his strange ships, horses, and weapons. He took possession of Tabasco, and they did not fight—instead they sent gifts.

Now create similar combinations for the following sets of simple sentences. On line e, add your own combination. Then select the one that best fits the given context.

1

SIMPLE SENTENCES:
He could not tolerate Princess Caroline.
This had a cause.
She never took a bath.

COMBINATIONS:
(a) _____
(b) _____
(c) _____
(d) _____
(e) _____

CONTEXT:
Later to become George IV of England, the prince had had many celebrated love affairs. Unfortunately, his affections did not extend to his new bride; _____even for a moment.

2

SIMPLE SENTENCES:
The dog was salivating at the sound of the metronome.
This had a cause.
Conditioning had taken place.

COMBINATIONS:
(a) _____
(b) _____

(c) _____
(d) _____
(e) _____

CONTEXT:

In careful experiments with a dog, Pavlov always sounded a metronome just before the animal received food. Later, he found that the dog would begin to produce saliva whenever the metronome sounded. Pavlov concluded that he had produced an artificial reflex: the reason the dog had salivated originally was that this was its natural reaction to food, but _____.

3

SIMPLE SENTENCES:

Bolts can now be tightened accurately.
This has a cause.
Torque wrenches measure rotary force.

COMBINATIONS:

(a) _____
(b) _____
(c) _____
(d) _____
(e) _____

CONTEXT:

Bolts are most effective when adjusted properly. The invention of the torque wrench has made their adjustment quite simple. _____ _____by even the most inexperienced mechanics. Some torque wrenches have a lighted dial; others produce an audible click. They indicate when the proper degree of tightness is reached.

4

Complete the list of simple sentences by filling in the blank. Then create a set of combinations as before.

SIMPLE SENTENCES:

Roommates often have disagreements.
This has a cause.

COMBINATIONS:

(a) _____

(b) _____

(c) _____

(d) _____

(e) _____

OPEN EXERCISE A

The following simple sentences constitute a short essay called "The Play's the Thing." Rewrite the sentences in essay form. (A gap between lines indicates that you should start a new paragraph.) You will notice that sentences 10–12, 19–21, and 35–37 are of the type you have worked with in the previous exercise. Compare your finished essay with those of your classmates and be prepared to discuss the choices you have made.

1. American students read William Shakespeare's plays.
2. They read at least one of them.
3. Few finish school without doing this.
4. The plays were written almost 400 years ago.
5. They were written by an Englishman.
6. Yet they are very much a part of our educational tradition.
7. Why is this so?

8. There is one best way to find the answer to this question.
9. It is to see one of Shakespeare's plays performed.
10. His plays reflect an instinct for what will work on stage.
11. This has a cause.
12. Shakespeare was an actor.
13. He knew what audiences liked.
14. He was the most popular playwright of his time.
15. It was an age when people went to the theater.
16. The people were of every class.
17. It was an age when plays were hooted off the stage.
18. This often happened.
19. Shakespeare's audience could appreciate the plays.
20. This had a cause.

21. He combined comedy with tragedy.

22. Something else has attracted people to Shakespeare's plays.
23. It is his knowledge of all kinds of people.
24. It is his knowledge of how they think.
25. It is his knowledge of how they feel.
26. This knowledge is unsurpassed.
27. Some of Shakespeare's characters are clowns.
28. Some of them are kings.
29. Understanding them has helped people understand themselves.
30. Shakespeare's characters are among the most convincing in literature.
31. They are among the most interesting in literature.
32. Cordelia's father is King Lear.
33. Cordelia refuses to flatter him.
34. Audiences care deeply when this happens.
35. Othello decides to kill Desdemona.
36. This has a cause.
37. He believes she was unfaithful to him.
38. Audiences care deeply when this happens as well.

39. There is another reason for Shakespeare's popularity.
40. It is his unrivaled command of language.
41. The poetry of his words can be unforgettable.
42. The power of his words can be unforgettable.
43. "A rose by any other name would smell as sweet."
44. "My kingdom for a horse!"
45. These are examples of quotations.
46. The quotations are from his plays.

47. Shakespeare's plays are performed today.
48. They are performed throughout the world.
49. We read his plays.
50. We study his plays.
51. We view his plays.
52. Doing these things has a result.
53. We keep the plays alive.
54. We do this for future generations.
55. They will be able to enjoy his plays as well.

MODELED EXERCISE B

SIMPLE SENTENCES:
Alexander Fleming saw the petri dish.
This had an effect.
He was greatly surprised.

COMBINATIONS:
(a) When Alexander Fleming saw the petri dish, he was greatly surprised.
(b) Alexander Fleming was greatly surprised when he saw the petri dish.
(c) Seeing the petri dish greatly surprised Alexander Fleming.
(d) As he saw the petri dish, Alexander Fleming was greatly surprised.

Select the combination that works best in the following context.

CONTEXT:
_____in which the bacteria had been growing. A mold had killed some of the bacteria. This accident led to the discovery of penicillin.

Now create similar combinations for the following sets of simple sentences. On line e, add your own combination. Then select the one that best fits the given context.

1

SIMPLE SENTENCES:
Children watch many acts of violence on T.V.
This has an effect.
The children are desensitized.

COMBINATIONS:
(a) _____
(b) _____
(c) _____
(d) _____
(e) _____

CONTEXT:
Studies show that _____and can cause them to become more violent adults.

2

SIMPLE SENTENCES:
Our corporations lose business to Japan.
This has an effect.
They are frightened.

COMBINATIONS:
(a) _____
(b) _____
(c) _____
(d) _____
(e) _____

CONTEXT:
The economic threat of Japan is such that when American companies lose business to Europe, they are annoyed, but _____.

3

SIMPLE SENTENCES:
The company president will near retirement age.
This will have an effect.
She will be newly challenged.

COMBINATIONS:
(a) _____
(b) _____
(c) _____
(d) _____
(e) _____

CONTEXT:
_____, who, like many successful entrepreneurs, fears that none of her subordinates will be able to run the company as she has.

4

Complete the simple sentences by filling in the blanks. Then create a set of combinations as before.

SIMPLE SENTENCES:
I heard _____.
This had an effect.
I was _____.

COMBINATIONS:
(a) _____
(b) _____
(c) _____
(d) _____
(e) _____

OPEN EXERCISE B

The following simple sentences constitute a short essay called "Lost: Four Billion Dollars." Rewrite the sentences in essay form. (A gap between lines indicates that you should start a new paragraph.) You will notice that sentences 1–3, 31–33, and 51–53 are of the type you have worked with in the previous exercise. Compare your finished essay with those of your classmates and be prepared to discuss the choices you have made.

1. People talk about finding buried treasure.
2. This has an effect.
3. Most of us laugh.
4. There may once have been chests buried underground.
5. The chests were filled with riches.
6. They have all been dug up by now.
7. We tend to believe this.
8. The fact is different.
9. Finding a buried treasure is a possibility.
10. It is not as outlandish as it seems.
11. "There is probably a total of four billion dollars.
12. It is hidden in spots.
13. The spots are various.
14. The spots are across the United States.
15. That is a conservative estimate."
16. That is what experienced treasure hunters say.

17. There are many legitimate treasures.
18. They have been lost.
19. They have never been found.
20. Some of them have stories behind them.
21. The stories are colorful.
22. Many people know the stories.
23. No one knows the locations of the treasures themselves.

24. The year was 1520.
25. Cortés was on his way.
26. Cortés was a Spanish adventurer.
27. His goal was to conquer the capital of the Aztecs.
28. The capital was rich.
29. It stood where Mexico City now stands.
30. Montezuma was the Aztec ruler.
31. He heard of Cortés's approach.
32. This had an effect.
33. He became worried.
34. He packed up a fortune in gold.
35. He sent it north by caravan.
36. The caravan was headed somewhere.
37. No one knows quite where.
38. Montezuma died during the Spanish conquest.
39. He left no word about the treasure.
40. People have been looking for it ever since.
41. They have looked as far north as New Mexico and Utah.

42. Jesse James and his gang also have a cache somewhere.
43. Jesse James was a western outlaw.
44. One of James's robberies yielded a fortune.
45. The fortune was in gold bullion.
46. They hid the fortune in the Wichita Mountains.
47. The Wichita Mountains are in the present state of Oklahoma.
48. Jesse James died.
49. His brother Frank bought a farm nearby.
50. Frank started to dig.
51. Frank might have remembered the spot.
52. This would have had a result.
53. He would have been one million dollars richer.
54. Frank's memory failed him, however.

55. The treasure is probably still buried.

56. There is apparently a washtub full of gold nuggets in Colorado.
57. There is apparently a copper box full of gold coins in Oklahoma.
58. There is apparently train robbery loot in Indiana.
59. There is apparently bank robbery money in Vermont.
60. They are all well-known treasures.
61. Some of them have been sought by thousands of people.
62. Many people have searched the most obvious sites.
63. This has had a result.
64. People may investigate old mine shafts.
65. People may investigate abandoned farm houses.
66. There is probably little to be gained from doing these things.
67. Something else is more likely.
68. Clues will be found by another kind of search.
69. The search will be through deeds.
70. The search will be through wills.
71. The search will be through old newspapers.
72. The files of libraries may reveal new information.
73. The files of courthouses may reveal new information.
74. The files are dusty.
75. The information could lead someone to buried treasure.

MODELED EXERCISE C

SIMPLE SENTENCES:
The Amazon rain forest supports our climate.
There is a reason for this.
It provides one-fifth of the earth's oxygen.

COMBINATIONS:
(a) The Amazon rain forest supports our climate because it provides one-fifth of the earth's oxygen.
(b) Because the Amazon rain forest provides one-fifth of the earth's oxygen, it supports our climate.
(c) Our climate is supported by the Amazon rain forest, which provides one-fifth of the earth's oxygen.
(d) By providing one-fifth of the earth's oxygen, the Amazon rain forest has the effect of supporting our climate.

Select the combination that works best in the following context.

CONTEXT:

Conservationists argue that development of the Amazon watershed should be undertaken with extreme care. Known as the "lungs of the world," _____. Without this oxygen, life itself could not continue.

Now create similar combinations for the following sets of simple sentences. On line e, add your own combination. Then select the one that best fits the given context.

1

SIMPLE SENTENCES:

The Viking space missions have disproved earlier theories of life on Mars.
There is a reason for this.
They found no canals on the planet's surface.

COMBINATIONS:

(a) _____

(b) _____

(c) _____

(d) _____

(e) _____

CONTEXT:

Because _____, many plausible science fiction stories have now been outdated. Such literary losses are an unfortunate side effect of scientific discovery.

2

SIMPLE SENTENCES:

The managerial revolution has changed American business.
There is a reason for this.
It has put professionals in charge.

COMBINATIONS:

(a) _____

(b) _____

(c) _____
(d) _____
(e) _____

CONTEXT:
The development sometimes called _____—replacing private owners with trained managers.

3

SIMPLE SENTENCES:
The plowing of grassland caused erosion.
There was a reason for this.
Plowing destroyed the roots that held the soil in place.

COMBINATIONS:
(a) _____
(b) _____
(c) _____
(d) _____
(e) _____

CONTEXT:
Millions of acres of farmland in the South were ruined by drought and dust storms during the early part of this century. Scientists now say that farming was itself a cause. _____and contributing to the awful conditions that became known as the Dustbowl.

4

Complete the simple sentences by filling in the blanks. Then create a set of combinations as before.

SIMPLE SENTENCES:
School food _____.
There is a reason for this.
It _____.

COMBINATIONS:
(a) _____
(b) _____

(c) _____
(d) _____
(e) _____

OPEN EXERCISE C

The following simple sentences constitute a short essay called "Mysteries of the Humpback Whale." Rewrite the sentences in essay form. (A gap between lines indicates that you should start a new paragraph.) You will notice that sentences 34–36, 51–53, and 59–61 are of the type you have worked with in the previous exercise. Compare your finished essay with those of your classmates and be prepared to discuss the choices you have made.

1. The largest of the whales are big creatures.
2. They are the biggest that ever roamed the earth.
3. They are four times the size of the largest dinosaur.
4. They are thirty times the weight of an elephant.
5. They boast appetites that match their size.
6. Even a small whale can put away half a ton of food.
7. It does this in a single day.
8. Such a small whale is the humpback.
9. The humpback grows to a mere 40 tons.

10. Humpbacks are known as great eaters.
11. They are known as great fasters as well.
12. There is a supply of tiny worms, snails, and shrimplike shellfish.
13. The shrimplike shellfish are called krill.
14. The supply is plentiful.
15. Humpbacks feed off this supply for most of the year.
16. They do it in the Arctic and Antarctic oceans.
17. The polar caps expand.
18. This happens during the cold months.
19. The expansion cuts the whales off from their food supply.
20. They are forced into long periods of starvation.
21. This happens while they migrate to warmer waters.
22. They migrate in order to mate.
23. Humpbacks may swim as far as 4,000 miles in four months.
24. They swim while living mostly off their stores of fat.

25. Their stores of fat are called blubber.
26. Marine scientists and whaling ships track these yearly migrations.
27. They have done so for hundreds of years.
28. Yet scientists are still puzzled by unanswered questions.
29. How do the whales keep to a true course?
30. The course is over thousands of miles.
31. Do humpbacks always return to their native waters?

32. Many theories have been advanced.
33. They answer these and other questions.
34. The theories are discarded.
35. There is a reason for this.
36. Careful research proves that they don't fit the facts.
37. Humpback whales follow the same routes every year.
38. The whales migrate to the same areas for the winter.
39. The whales return without fail to their native waters.
40. Scientists believed these things until recently.
41. Then came a discovery.
42. It was amazing for the facts it revealed.
43. It was amazing for the way it was made.
44. There were two teams of researchers.
45. They were some 3,000 miles apart.
46. Both had been recording the singing of humpbacks.
47. The singing is underwater.
48. The teams compared tapes.
49. They found the songs were the same.
50. They found this to their astonishment.
51. This finding was completely unexpected.
52. There is a reason for this.
53. Different schools of humpback whales usually sing different songs.
54. There could be only one explanation.
55. Members of the two whale groups had come into contact with one another.
56. The researchers promptly set to work.
57. They worked on a new theory of whale migration.

58. Researchers take discoveries like these in good humor.
59. Scientists learn what they can through close observation at sea.
60. There is a reason for this.
61. Whales are too big to be brought into a laboratory.

62. These scientists are used to encountering the unexpected.
63. "These animals are strange.
64. They sometimes seem like visitors from another planet.
65. They seem just as foreign.
66. They seem just as mysterious, too."
67. Scientists say this.

MODELED EXERCISE D

SIMPLE SENTENCES:
You may use a shortwave radio.
This will have a result.
You can receive foreign radio broadcasts.

COMBINATIONS:
(a) The result of your using a shortwave radio is that you can receive foreign radio broadcasts.
(b) By using a shortwave radio, you can receive foreign radio broadcasts.
(c) You can receive foreign radio broadcasts if you use a shortwave radio.
(d) By using a shortwave radio to receive foreign radio broadcasts, you. . . .

Select the combination that works best in the following context.

CONTEXT:
Seeing things from other points of view is always instructive. _____ _____can gain some new perspectives on current events.

Now create similar combinations for the following sets of simple sentences. On line e, add your own combination. Then select the one that best fits the given context.

1

SIMPLE SENTENCES:
You may stay close to the floor.
This will have a result.
You can lessen the risk of smoke inhalation.

COMBINATIONS:

(a) _____

(b) _____

(c) _____

(d) _____

(e) _____

CONTEXT:

By covering your mouth with a wet cloth and _____ during a fire.

2

SIMPLE SENTENCES:

Vegetarians may choose foods carefully.
This will have a result.
They can receive adequate protein.

COMBINATIONS:

(a) _____

(b) _____

(c) _____

(d) _____

(e) _____

CONTEXT:

It is difficult to obtain the right protein when one abstains from meat. However, _____ and follow the guidelines laid down by dietary research. The right combination of incomplete proteins—for example, beans and rice—can be equivalent to the complete protein found in meat.

3

SIMPLE SENTENCES:

People might learn to control the weather.
This would have a result.
They could use droughts and storms as weapons.

COMBINATIONS:

(a) _____

(b) _____

(c) _____
(d) _____
(e) _____

CONTEXT:

Climate control is generally thought of as a desirable goal. But it could have some unfortunate results. _____, for example. This seems an awe-inspiring possibility, especially when one considers the violence of tornados and hurricanes.

4

Complete the simple sentence by filling in the blank. Then create a set of combinations as before.

SIMPLE SENTENCES:

You may not get enough sleep.
This can have a result.
You can _____.

COMBINATIONS:

(a) _____
(b) _____
(c) _____
(d) _____
(e) _____

OPEN EXERCISE D

The following simple sentences constitute a short essay called "Community Colleges on the Rise." Sentences 43 through 50 are missing; you will have to supply these yourself. (The general topic of the sentences you write should be the drawbacks that community colleges have for certain people. Feel free to add more or fewer than the specified number of sentences if you think that doing so will improve the essay.)

Rewrite the sentences in essay form. (A gap between lines indicates that you should start a new paragraph.) You will notice that sentences

22–24 and 57–59 are of the type you have worked with in the previous exercise. Some of the sentences you supply should be of this type as well.

Compare your finished essay with those of your classmates and be prepared to discuss the choices you have made.

1. The birth rate is down.
2. College costs are up.
3. Four-year colleges will be facing some difficult times ahead.
4. The future looks rosy for some colleges, however.
5. These are two-year community colleges.
6. Some community colleges are having to turn away students.
7. There is a reason for this.
8. The reason is that so many students want admission to community colleges.
9. This is a fact.

10. Some college students are freshmen and sophomores.
11. Fifty-three percent of them now attend community colleges.
12. Community colleges have grown in popularity.
13. A number of reasons explain this growth.

14. Community colleges stress career training.
15. Today's students are job-oriented.
16. Career training is popular with such students.
17. It is more popular than the liberal arts program.
18. The liberal arts program is traditional.
19. Career training may be available at four-year colleges.
20. It costs far less at community colleges.
21. The time needed for career training is also less.
22. Students may want to enter the work force.
23. This will have a result.
24. They may not want to wait four years.
25. Community colleges offer programs.
26. The programs vary in length.
27. The range is from a few months to two years.

28. Community college students vary in age.
29. The range is from teenagers to older adults.

30. The average age is 27.
31. This age range provides an interesting mix.
32. The mix is in the classroom.
33. Community colleges are convenient for older students.
34. They offer evening classes.
35. They offer part-time programs.
36. This is important to certain students.
37. These students already have jobs.
38. These students already have family responsibilities.

39. Community colleges are not for everyone.
40. This is certain.
41. Some people have needs.
42. Two-year colleges cannot fill these needs.
43. _____
44. _____
45. _____
46. _____
47. _____
48. _____
49. _____
50. _____
51. Some of these people would be better off at four-year colleges.
52. Some would be better off not going to college at all.

53. Community colleges may have drawbacks.
54. Even so, the following is true.
55. Community colleges have a strong appeal.
56. Their appeal is for today's generation of students.
57. The job market may continue to tighten.
58. This will have a result.
59. Community colleges will grow more popular still.
60. This is probable.

PART THREE:
EDITING

INTRODUCTION

The French novelist Gustave Flaubert (1821–1880) is legendary for the intense effort he put into his writing. Never willing to commit to paper anything that he felt was less than perfect, Flaubert would search endlessly for the exact word or phrase that would express his ideas. It generally took him a week to write a single page, and his best-known book, *Madame Bovary,* took more than four years to complete.

Unfortunately, most of us have neither the time nor the patience to demand such perfection in our own work. The average writer's first draft includes a reasonable number of unnecessary words and ideas, badly-ordered paragraphs, grammatical errors, imprecise sentences, and sentences that make no sense at all. This is true even of professional writers—who, like you, often have to write under pressure and may not be entirely sure of what they're saying until their words hit the paper. Most well-known pieces of writing, in fact, began their existence in forms quite different from those we now take for granted. For example, here is how the famous last sentence of the Gettysburg Address looked in Abraham Lincoln's first draft:

> It is rather for us, the living, we here be dedicated to the great task remaining before us—that, from these honored dead we take increased devotion to that cause for which they here, gave the last full measure of devotion—that we here highly resolve these dead shall not have died in vain; that the nation, shall have a new birth of freedom, and that government of the people by the people for the people, shall not perish from the earth.

We may safely presume that Lincoln's speech would not have become quite so famous if its last sentence had been delivered in this form. Not only does it sound clumsy and unnatural (partly because of misplaced or omitted punctuation, partly because of some awkward word placement), but the first part of the sentence is completely incoherent. While it is not true, as commonly believed, that Lincoln wrote this first draft on the back of an envelope, it is clear that Lincoln was more concerned at this stage with what he wanted to *say* in the speech than with small details of style.

You, like most writers, are probably closer to Lincoln than to Flaubert. You've already discovered how many different things you have to keep track of when you write—the meaning of your words, the structure of your sentences, the relationship between your style and your purpose—and, like Lincoln, you probably find it difficult to think about all of these things at the same time. Fortunately, it's almost never *necessary* to think about all of these things simultaneously. Once you've completed a draft that says what you want it to say, you're free to go back as many times as necessary to improve the way you've said it.

This process of making improvements in grammar and style is known as *editing* your work. In many cases, a writer needs to edit only once—having found the weak spots in one draft, he or she can write another draft that solves the stylistic problems. In other cases, several more drafts may be needed. Lincoln, in fact, wrote five drafts of the Gettysburg Address before he was satisfied. Each draft contained only minor changes, but the difference between the first and the last is striking. By improving his punctuation, adding and deleting words, and shifting the order of certain phrases, Lincoln was able to express the same thoughts in a much more memorable way. Compare the last sentence of his final draft with the first-draft version on page 195:

It is rather for us to be here dedicated to the great task remaining before us—that from these honored dead we take increased devotion to that cause for which they gave the last full measure of devotion—that we here highly resolve that these dead shall not have died in vain—that this nation, under God, shall have a new birth of freedom—and that government of the people, by the people, for the people, shall not perish from the earth.

Writing teachers are fond of saying that a first draft is not "engraved in stone"—meaning, of course, that any or all of it can easily be changed later on if the writer is willing to make the effort. Lincoln had no way of knowing that his Gettysburg Address *would* someday be engraved in stone, as it is today in the Lincoln Memorial, but we may be thankful that he was willing to take the time to make it worthy of the honor. While you may never write anything quite as historic, your readers will be equally thankful for the time you spend in making your final draft as readable as possible.

DECOMBINING AND RECOMBINING

Anyone who has ever repaired a piece of machinery knows that there are two basic processes involved: taking the machine apart and putting it together again. Imagine, for instance, that you have noticed a strange rattling sound coming from inside your vacuum cleaner. Having hit, kicked, and shaken the vacuum cleaner without any noticeable result, you reluctantly decide to take it apart piece by piece until you find the source of the noise. First of all, you look for the places where bolts are most likely to be hidden: next to seams, beneath plastic panels, or on the underside. Then, having found the right place to start, you begin to take the machine apart. In order to remove each new part, you have to find out how it's connected to the part it's attached to.

Once you've found the problem—a dime, let's say, that found its way into the motor housing—you are faced with the most difficult task of all: putting the vacuum cleaner *back together*. Do you remember where each part belongs? Can you assemble them neatly and securely? And, most important, will the vacuum cleaner still work when you've finished the job? The answers to these questions will depend partly upon how careful you were in taking the machine apart, and partly upon how much you know about vacuum cleaners and how they work.

Don't worry—we haven't forgotten that this is a writing book rather than a manual on appliance repair. The reason we've included this discussion of nuts and bolts is that fixing an awkward sentence is, in many ways, like repairing a rattling vacuum cleaner. A resourceful writer can take any sentence apart, correct its problems, and put the sentence back together again so that it works better than it did before.

The modeled exercises you completed in Part Two showed you how simple sentences could be combined into more complex sentences. As you discovered, however, some combinations will work better than others in a particular context—and some combinations won't work at all. In Part Three, you'll encounter a new kind of modeled exercise in which you'll be asked to *de*combine a problem sentence. Then, using your knowledge from Parts One and Two, you'll be able to *re*combine the sentence to make it work better than before.

Each section of these new exercises will begin—rather than end—with a context paragraph. Somewhere in the paragraph will be a sentence (or part of a sentence) that just doesn't sound quite right. The "rattling" sentence will be highlighted in bold type, as it is in the following example:

CONTEXT:
Despite its syncopated rhythms, ragtime was closely related in structure to the romantic piano music being heard in concert halls. Ragtime was not, however, considered "serious" music; it retained its second-class status throughout the career of its greatest composer. **Writing the first ragtime opera, respectability—which he sought—was never attained by Scott Joplin.** When he died, in 1917, he was bankrupt and forgotten.

Just beneath the context paragraph, you'll find a model that shows how the boldface sentence can be broken down into simple sentences. For the sentence about Scott Joplin, the model would look like this:

SIMPLE SENTENCES:
1. Scott Joplin wrote the first ragtime opera.
2. He sought respectability.
3. He never attained it.

Then you'll come to another model showing how the simple sentences might be recombined in better ways. This part of the exercise looks just like the models in Part Two, except that there are only three combinations instead of four.

RECOMBINATIONS:
(a) Scott Joplin, who wrote the first ragtime opera, never attained the respectability he sought.
(b) Scott Joplin wrote the first ragtime opera; he sought respectability but never attained it.
(c) Scott Joplin, who never attained the respectability he sought, wrote the first ragtime opera.

Finally, you'll see a familiar request in a slightly unfamiliar form:

*Select the combination that works best in the preceding context.*_____

[Although (a), (b), and (c) are *all* better than the original boldface sentence, we think you'll agree that the combination that fits best here is (a).]

As in Part Two, this first section of the exercise is followed by several numbered sections in which you are asked to imitate the model. Here, however, your task is harder—as you'll see in the following example:

Now create a similar set of simple sentences from the words printed in bold type and combine the simple sentences in the ways shown in the model. On line d, add your own combination. Then select the one that best fits the given context.

1

CONTEXT:
Making promises, political candidates can't always keep them; they often run on personality alone. An example is Dwight D. Eisenhower, whose image as a war hero so overshadowed his political beliefs that he was courted by both the Democratic and the Republican parties.

SIMPLE SENTENCES:
1. _____
2. _____
3. _____

RECOMBINATIONS:
(a) _____
(b) _____
(c) _____
(d) _____

*Select the combination that works best in the preceding context.*_____

According to the directions, the first thing you have to do is decombine the sentence in bold type to create a set of simple sentences. You'll notice, however, that the sentence about political candidates is put together quite differently from the Scott Joplin sentence in the model— its word order is entirely different, and it includes a semicolon that the original sentence didn't have. Nevertheless, the set of simple sentences that you derive from it should be just like the set of simple sentences in the model. There is no formula for doing this; you'll have to let the *meaning* of the sentence be your guide.

You know, for instance, that the sentence you're working with is generally about political candidates. You'll also find that the word **promises** behaves very much like the word **respectability** did in the model. Once you've made these observations, you need only to sort the pieces out in the proper order. To make the solution clear, we'll show you the model on the left and the new sentences on the right:

1. Scott Joplin wrote the first ragtime opera.	1. Political candidates often run on personality alone.
2. He sought respectability.	2. They make promises.
3. He never attained it.	3. They can't always keep them.

The next step is to combine these sentences in the ways you were shown in the model. Since you've had so much practice doing this sort of thing in Part Two, we won't bother with a side-by-side display. The solution, which you should be able to reach quite easily, is as follows:

(a) Political candidates, who often run on personality alone, can't always keep the promises they make.
(b) Political candidates often run on personality alone; they make promises but can't always keep them.
(c) Political candidates, who can't always keep the promises they make, often run on personality alone.
(d) [Your choice]

All that is left for you to do is to choose the combination that works best in the original context. In this case it is (c), unless your own combination (d) works better.

CORRECTING ERRORS

A point we've made quite often throughout the book is that many stylistic decisions are neither "right" nor "wrong"—they are simply matters of judgment, in which one person's opinion may easily differ from another's. Perhaps it is time for us to make the opposite point:

many stylistic decisions *are* wrong, and it is up to you as a writer to correct these decisions.

Even the most experienced writers are prone to make grammatical errors when they experiment with unusual ways of putting sentences together. They may arrange words in the wrong order, use the wrong forms of particular words, misuse punctuation marks, or leave out some important punctuation marks altogether. (Look back at the first draft of the Gettysburg Address, which exhibits many such problems.) There is nothing wrong with making mistakes like these when you write—so long as you are prepared to locate and correct them when you've finished your draft.

Of course, the only way you can correct a grammatical error is to realize that you've made one in the first place. For this reason, we recommend that you get hold of a standard writer's handbook and refer to it whenever you're in doubt about the correctness of a sentence you've written. If the handbook indicates that you've made an error, you can use the techniques of sentence decombining and recombining to correct the problem.

This book, as you know by now, is not a grammar book; we have neither the space nor the inclination to burden you with lists of do's and don'ts. What we can do, however, is show you what some common grammatical errors look like and how they can be eliminated. The following set of exercises will show you how certain errors can be corrected creatively; it will then be up to you to apply this same creativity to whatever grammatical problems you find in your own writing.

Remember, the blank lines are for illustration only. Do all your work on a separate sheet of paper. Don't write in the book.

MODELED EXERCISE A

CONTEXT:
When it was clear that Germany would lose the war, many high-ranking Nazis fled their country and went into hiding. Years later, **a worldwide search was conducted by Israeli agents to locate those Nazis who**

had escaped, capturing Adolf Eichmann was one of its highest priorities. As overseer of the so-called "final solution," Eichmann had played a major role in the deaths of millions of Jews.

SIMPLE SENTENCES:
1. Israeli agents conducted a worldwide search.
2. Its purpose was to locate those Nazis who had escaped.
3. Capturing Adolf Eichmann was one of its highest priorities.

RECOMBINATIONS:
(a) A worldwide search was conducted by Israeli agents to locate those Nazis who had escaped, and capturing Adolf Eichmann was one of its highest priorities.
(b) Capturing Adolf Eichmann was one of the highest priorities of a worldwide search. It was conducted by Israeli agents to locate those Nazis who had escaped.
(c) Israeli agents conducted a worldwide search, with capturing Adolf Eichmann as one of its highest priorities, to locate those Nazis who had escaped.

Select the combination that works best in the preceding context._____

Now create a similar set of simple sentences from the words printed in bold type and combine the simple sentences in the ways shown in the model. On line d, add your own combination. Then select the one that best fits the given context.

1

CONTEXT:
Colleges are usually thought of as peaceful centers of learning, but, in the 1960s, **student groups held antiwar demonstrations to bring an end to the Vietnam conflict, college campuses were frequently their sites,** and they are credited by many historians with helping to turn American public opinion against the war.

SIMPLE SENTENCES:
1. _____
2. _____
3. _____

RECOMBINATIONS:

(a) _____

(b) _____

(c) _____

(d) _____

Select the combination that works best in the preceding context. ____

2

CONTEXT:
In response to increasing scientific interest in parapsychology, **Dr. J.B. Rhine was the head of a research program conducted by Duke University, its purpose was to investigate the existence of ESP** and to test new theories concerning clairvoyance, telepathy, and telekinesis.

SIMPLE SENTENCES:

1. _____

2. _____

3. _____

RECOMBINATIONS:

(a) _____

(b) _____

(c) _____

(d) _____

Select the combination that works best in the preceding context. ____

3

CONTEXT:
Jomo Kenyatta was one of the primary forces in Kenya's transition from a British colony to an independent country. In 1952, **a terrorist group called the Mau Mau was formed by the Kikuyu tribe to force whites from Kenya, Kenyatta was its leader.** Although he was imprisoned a year later, Kenyatta emerged in 1963 to become the first prime minister of an independent Kenya.

SIMPLE SENTENCES:

1. _____
2. _____
3. _____

RECOMBINATIONS:

(a) _____
(b) _____
(c) _____
(d) _____

Select the combination that works best in the preceding context._____

OPEN EXERCISE A

The following is a draft of a short essay. The sentences printed in bold type are similar to those you worked with in the previous exercise. Revise these sentences so that they work well in the context of the essay. Compare your solutions with those of your classmates and be prepared to discuss the choices you have made.

America's Manifest Destiny

Long before America's aggressive expansion got underway in the 1840s, people had dreamed of one great nation extending from sea to sea. The term "manifest destiny" came into popular use in the mid-1840s as a way to express that dream. The phrase implied that it was God's intention to set aside the American continent for free development by U.S. citizens. No outside force or physical barrier could be allowed to stop their expansion from the Atlantic to the Pacific and from Canada to the Rio Grande.

The idea, which had great appeal for the American public, was used by politicians to rally support for their campaigns, Presidential candidate James Polk was one of its greatest advocates. He was an eager expansionist, absolutely committed to the annexation of Texas. By conducting a "manifest destiny" campaign, he won the election of 1844.

"Manifest destiny" was also used by economic expansionists to justify extending U.S. territorial borders, the acquisition of Pacific ports was their goal. They argued that California and Oregon had to be added to the republic. Otherwise, European powers might gain a foothold on the west coast and thus dominate trade with the Orient.

The decade of the 1840s was one of tremendous growth. The United States gained more territory in this single decade than ever before or since. When it was over, America's borders did indeed reflect her "manifest destiny."

MODELED EXERCISE B

CONTEXT:
The launch of the Russian satellite Sputnik. People tend to remember it, because it signaled the beginning of the U.S.-Soviet space race. However, a similar launch that took place late in 1982 has gone almost unnoticed—despite the fact that it may trigger an even more important competition in space. The Conestoga 1, a 37-foot rocket, was launched by a private American company that hopes to break the U.S. government's monopoly on carrying payloads into space.

SIMPLE SENTENCES:
1. People tend to remember the launch of the Russian satellite Sputnik.
2. They remember for a reason.
3. It signaled the beginning of the U.S.-Soviet space race.

RECOMBINATIONS:
(a) People tend to remember the launch of the Russian satellite Sputnik because it signaled the beginning of the U.S.-Soviet space race.
(b) Because it signaled the beginning of the U.S.-Soviet space race, people tend to remember the launch of the Russian satellite Sputnik.
(c) The launch of the Russian satellite Sputnik signaled the beginning of the U.S.-Soviet space race, so people tend to remember it.

*Select the combination that works best in the preceding context.*_____

Now create a similar set of simple sentences from the words printed in bold type and combine the simple sentences in the ways shown in the model. On line d, add your own combination. Then select the one that best fits the given context.

1

CONTEXT:

Children are very observant of the world around them. Although we may tell children that all jobs are open to both sexes, they see plenty of evidence to the contrary in their daily lives. **A girl may be hesitant to enter a traditionally male career because of what it offers. Few female role models.** Likewise, a boy is unlikely to want to become a homemaker—simply because he has never *seen* a male homemaker.

SIMPLE SENTENCES:

1. _____
2. _____
3. _____

RECOMBINATIONS:

(a) _____
(b) _____
(c) _____
(d) _____

*Select the combination that works best in the preceding context.*_____

2

CONTEXT:

If you have a limited clothing budget, it pays to select your wardrobe carefully. **You may want to avoid spending money on trendy fashions. Because they date. Quickly.** You should also consider avoiding "designer label" garments altogether. They give you very little value for your money.

SIMPLE SENTENCES:

1. _____
2. _____
3. _____

RECOMBINATIONS:
(a) _____
(b) _____
(c) _____
(d) _____

*Select the combination that works best in the preceding context.*_____

3

CONTEXT:
The world of popular music pays very little attention to Randy Newman. On account of his songs, which are not considered "commercial." And because Newman is quite a cynical artist, he pays equally little attention to the world of popular music.

SIMPLE SENTENCES:
1. _____
2. _____
3. _____

RECOMBINATIONS:
(a) _____
(b) _____
(c) _____
(d) _____

*Select the combination that works best in the preceding context.*_____

OPEN EXERCISE B

The following is a draft of a short essay. The sentences and fragments printed in bold type are similar to those you worked with in the previous exercise. Revise them so that they work well in the context of the essay. Compare your solutions with those of your classmates and be prepared to discuss the choices you have made.

The Dust Bowl

A combination of little rain and bad farming practices brought years of dust storms to the Great Plains states. The 1920s had been a time of plentiful rain, but a period of drought began in 1930. In addition, the farmlands themselves had been overworked. **The soil could no longer support healthy crops because of overplanting. Years of it. It stripped the soil of its nutrients.** The undernourished crops with their poor root systems did little to hold the topsoil in place. The soil turned dry and powdery, and the wind blew it away.

Farmers in the Dust Bowl states—Kansas, Oklahoma, and Texas— were amazed at what they saw. **Heavy clouds of dust in the air. Because the clouds blocked out the sun, streetlights were kept burning all day.** One Texas man recorded going 27 days in one month without being able to see across the street.

Families had to abandon their farms. Because there was nothing left but rocky subsoil, in which no crop would grow. Most people left for California, where they had heard there were good jobs and good farming. But there were far more hungry migrants than there were jobs. Government programs eventually helped the farmers improve their methods. But for many, it was too late. Their farmlands had blown away.

MODELED EXERCISE C

CONTEXT:
When bodies were found in the wet, spongy bogs of Sweden and Denmark, they were thought to be victims of recent murders. They turned out instead to be prehistoric sacrifices to the gods. **Thrown into the bogs thousands of years ago, a natural ingredient in the bog water had preserved the bodies**—tannic acid, the chemical used to tan leather.

SIMPLE SENTENCES:
1. The bodies were thrown into the bogs.
2. This happened thousands of years ago.
3. A natural ingredient in the bog water had preserved them.

RECOMBINATIONS:

(a) The bodies, thrown into the bogs thousands of years ago, had been preserved by a natural ingredient in the bog water.

(b) A natural ingredient in the bog water had preserved the bodies, which were thrown into the bogs thousands of years ago.

(c) The bodies were thrown into the bogs thousands of years ago; a natural ingredient in the bog water had preserved them.

*Select the combination that works best in the preceding context.*_____

Now create a similar set of simple sentences from the words printed in bold type and combine the simple sentences in the ways shown in the model. On line d, add your own combination. Then select the one that best fits the given context.

1

CONTEXT:

In ancient Greek mythology, the river Styx had the power to make a person immortal. The son of a goddess and an ordinary man, **a poisoned arrow nevertheless killed Achilles, dipped into the river soon after he was born.** The arrow hit the heel by which Achilles' mother had held him when she immersed him, upside-down, in the Styx.

SIMPLE SENTENCES:

1. _____
2. _____
3. _____

RECOMBINATIONS:

(a) _____
(b) _____
(c) _____
(d) _____

*Select the combination that works best in the preceding context.*_____

2

CONTEXT:
Over a million people visit the Statue of Liberty each year. Thirty people at a time can gather in the statue's crown, where a row of windows offers a panoramic view of the New York harbor. **The statue's arm can be entered only by maintenance workers, closed to the public for reasons of safety** about 65 years ago.

SIMPLE SENTENCES:
1. _____
2. _____
3. _____

RECOMBINATIONS:
(a) _____
(b) _____
(c) _____
(d) _____

Select the combination that works best in the preceding context. _____

3

CONTEXT:
Almost nothing is known about the strange disappearance of the American writer Ambrose Bierce. **Last seen headed for Mexico in 1913, no one ever found Bierce.** Although he is rumored to have been killed by Mexican revolutionaries, no evidence of murder has come to light. Reference books, lacking more specific information, list Bierce's death date as "about 1914."

SIMPLE SENTENCES:
1. _____
2. _____
3. _____

RECOMBINATIONS:
(a) _____
(b) _____

(c) _____ .
(d) _____

*Select the combination that works best in the preceding context.*_____

OPEN EXERCISE C

The following is a draft of a short essay. The sentences printed in bold type are similar to those you worked with in the previous exercise. Revise these sentences so that they work well in the context of the essay. Compare your solutions with those of your classmates and be prepared to discuss the choices you have made.

A Good Idea Gone Wrong

Virtually every failure that ever occurred has started out as somebody's "good idea." No one, after all, sets out to create a disaster. Unfortunately, simple good intentions are never a guarantee of success— **attractive at the beginning, poor planning often destroys so-called "good ideas."** One example of how this can happen involves a French scientist named Leopold Trovelot.

Trovelot wanted to make money. **Impressed by the success of the European silk industry, an idea struck him.** The United States, he knew, had to import nearly all of its silk from abroad; sillkworms were difficult to cultivate in America, where the mulberry leaves that silkworms eat are scarce. Trovelot's idea was to breed a new kind of silkworm that would be especially suited to the United States. The new insect—a cross between a silkworm and a European caterpillar— would spin silk, but it would be much hardier than an ordinary silkworm. In addition, it would eat common oak leaves rather than mulberry leaves.

Trovelot came to Massachusetts in 1869, bringing with him a cage of European caterpillars. Before he was able to make much progress with his experiments, some of his caterpillars—also known as gypsy moths—managed to escape from their cage. They immediately set out to find some oak leaves.

Today, gypsy moths are found all over the Northeast. They destroyed nine million acres of forest in 1981. **Free of natural enemies in North America, other insects do not threaten them;** their population has continued to increase steadily. Attempts to control gypsy moths with pesticides have been unsuccessful. (Very potent pesticides, such as DDT, *can* kill gypsy moths, but they kill a great many beneficial creatures as well. The use of DDT was banned in the 1960s.) Other methods of control, such as burning the gypsy moths' eggs, have had little overall effect.

Trovelot's "good idea" failed in more ways than one. More than a century later, America continues to be the world's largest importer of silk.

MODELED EXERCISE D

CONTEXT:
After a dispute with Buffalo Bill, Annie Oakley and her husband split off from the Wild West Show and went on their own tour of Europe. In Germany, **Oakley attempted to shoot a cigarette that was held in the crown prince's lips, and it was successful.** This stunt, along with Oakley's other sharpshooting tricks, fascinated the Germans—especially the prince, who later became the infamous Kaiser Wilhelm of World War I.

SIMPLE SENTENCES:
1. Oakley attempted to shoot a cigarette.
2. The cigarette was held in the crown prince's lips.
3. Her attempt was successful.

RECOMBINATIONS:
(a) Oakley's attempt to shoot a cigarette that was held in the crown prince's lips was successful.
(b) Oakley attempted to shoot a cigarette that was held in the crown prince's lips, and her attempt was successful.
(c) Oakley's attempt—which was successful—was to shoot a cigarette that was held in the crown prince's lips.

*Select the combination that works best in the preceding context.*___

Now create a similar set of simple sentences from the words printed in bold type and combine the simple sentences in the ways shown in the model. On line d, add your own combination. Then select the one that best fits the given context.

1

CONTEXT:
In 1912, the United States Treasury came up with a novel way to conserve funds. **The Treasury decided to wash soiled bills that were turned in by banks, and it was later reversed.** Objections were raised soon afterwards by Secret Service agents, who found that the washed bills were hard to distinguish from counterfeit bills.

SIMPLE SENTENCES:

1. _____
2. _____
3. _____

RECOMBINATIONS:

(a) _____
(b) _____
(c) _____
(d) _____

*Select the combination that works best in the preceding context.*_____

2

CONTEXT:
Sitting Bull refused to obey the government's order that all Indians return to their reservations, and it resulted in military violence. The U.S. Army mounted an expedition against the Indians, and Sitting Bull prepared his own army to face the government troops. After the battle of Little Bighorn, in which General George A. Custer and his entire battalion were killed, Sitting Bull fled to Canada to avoid U.S. retaliation. He lived there, in poverty, until 1881.

SIMPLE SENTENCES:

1. _____
2. _____
3. _____

RECOMBINATIONS:
(a) _____
(b) _____
(c) _____
(d) _____

Select the combination that works best in the preceding context._____

3

CONTEXT:
The man most responsible for modern traffic regulations never drove a car. As early as 1900, **William Eno was disgusted with the traffic that clogged New York City streets, and it eventually led him to write an article about it.** Titled "Reform in Our Street Traffic Urgently Needed," the article established him as a safety expert. After helping to develop methods of traffic control in the United States, Eno became a consultant overseas. In Paris, he developed a plan for traffic flow around the Arch of Triumph.

SIMPLE SENTENCES:
1. _____
2. _____
3. _____

RECOMBINATIONS:
(a) _____
(b) _____
(c) _____
(d) _____

Select the combination that works best in the preceding context._____

OPEN EXERCISE D

The following is a draft of a short essay. The sentences printed in bold type are similar to those you worked with in the previous exercise. Revise these sentences so that they work well in the context of the essay. Compare your solutions with those of your classmates and be prepared to discuss the choices you have made.

The Mystery of Amelia Earhart

In 1937, Amelia Earhart was ready to realize her dream of flying around the world. In May of that year, she began her trip by flying from Oakland, California, to Miami, Florida. Then, on June 1, she took off again—accompanied by a former Pan Am pilot named Frederick Noonan—and flew south. Their plan was to fly to Puerto Rico, Brazil, Africa, Pakistan, Burma, Singapore, Australia, New Guinea, Howland Island, Hawaii, and then back to Oakland. Earhart and Noonan arrived in New Guinea on June 30. Two days later, they left for Howland Island—where a Coast Guard cutter, the *Ithasca,* was waiting for them. On July 3, the *Isthasca* received a message from Earhart in which she reported cloudy weather, but most of the message was drowned out by static. Later messages reported that the plane's fuel was running low. **The *Ithasca* attempted to take a bearing on Earhart's position, but it was unsuccessful.** Shortly afterward, the cutter received a message from Earhart that gave her approximate position. That was the last message Earhart sent.

After waiting awhile longer near Howland Island, the *Ithasca* headed northwest toward the spot where Earhart and Noonan were believed to have gone down. Later, a $4 million task force—including a battleship, a carrier, and 60 planes—searched for three weeks over an area of 250,000 square miles. The task force found no trace of Earhart's plane, and the official conclusion was that Earhart and Noonan had run out of fuel, plunged into the ocean, and drowned.

Then, in 1944, a United States army officer discovered the wreckage of an American plane on the Japanese-held island of Saipan. The plane looked like Earhart's, and it proved to be marked with her registry number. U.S. marines also found a suitcase that contained a woman's clothing and a diary with Earhart's name on the cover. Most interestingly, U.S. military personnel who entered Tokyo at the end of World War II found a file there on Earhart. The file, however, has mysteriously disappeared—along with other evidence.

In 1960, a CBS newsman named Fred Goerner took up the search for Amelia Earhart. **Goerner decided to track down evidence that had been lost for years, and it turned into a grueling six-year investigation.** On the basis of his research, Goerner concluded that Earhart and

Noonan had been on a secret mission to report on Japanese military installations for the U.S. government. At the end of the mission, they had gotten lost, run out of fuel, and crash-landed in the Marshall Islands. They were then captured by the Japanese, taken to Saipan, and eventually killed.

Goerner has pressed for a Congressional inquiry into the case, but no one in Washington has been willing to take the initiative. **The government has failed to conduct an investigation that might clear up the matter once and for all, and it ensures that the disappearance of Amelia Earhart will remain a mystery.**

POLISHING

Despite all our talk about awkward sentences and grammatical errors, this part of the book was not intended to make you gloomy. If you've carefully planned a piece of writing and used good judgment in putting it together, there's a good chance that you won't have to do very much else. As you read through your first draft, you may find that, overall, it works quite well: it makes sense, it contains a minimum number of errors, and it accomplishes its purpose. If all that is indeed the case, feel free to make the necessary corrections, type up a final draft, and breathe a sigh of relief.

On the other hand, you may want to pause and give some thought to a maxim often repeated by writers: "No piece of writing is *ever* finished." Almost everyone who rereads a piece of work weeks or years later will find something that he or she would have said differently; to do so is an unavoidable part of being human. You're more likely to be satisfied with your work, however, if you take the time to read your "final" draft again with an eye toward *polishing* what you've written.

The following group of exercises will give you a chance to experiment with the sorts of changes that you might want to make at the polishing stage. As before, there are sentences in bold type that you'll be asked to decombine and then recombine. This time, however, you'll probably find nothing wrong—at least in a grammatical sense—with the sentences you're decombining. These sentences say exactly what they need to say, and they do so without making any outright errors.

Nevertheless, each of the boldface sentences is *unsatisfactory* in some way. Some of them sound awkward, some fit badly in their contexts, and some use too many words to express their ideas. All of these problems can be solved by the same process of decombining and recombining. In many cases, you'll find more than one problem in the same sentence (for instance, awkwardness and wordiness). You'll often be able to solve at least one of these problems even *before* you decombine—possibly by making a minor word change, such as turning **not unhappy** into **happy.** The models, as usual, will show you how.

By now, you've had so much practice in sentence combining—not to mention decombining and recombining—that you may find it possible to take shortcuts. In the open exercises, for instance, you may find it possible to rewrite the boldface sentences without having to take them apart and put them back together. You may simply know, intuitively, what sort of sentence would work best in that particular context. If that's the case—and if, when you review your solutions in class, you confirm that your shortcuts really do work—then go ahead and use them. Sentence combining, after all, is not an end in itself; it is simply a tool that can help you develop your intuition and thus become a better writer.

MODELED EXERCISE A

CONTEXT:
In the cities of the future, buses and cars may share the streets much more efficiently than they do today. **Transportation planners envision streets in which there are buses, and the buses are assigned to special lanes; the buses could control traffic lights**—insuring a green light at every corner.

SIMPLE SENTENCES:
1. Transportation planners envision streets.
2. In the streets are buses.
3. The buses are assigned to special lanes.
4. The buses could control traffic lights.

RECOMBINATIONS:
(a) Transportation planners envision streets in which buses, assigned to special lanes, could control traffic lights.
(b) Buses, assigned to special lanes, could control traffic lights in the streets envisioned by transportation planners.
(c) Streets envisioned by transportation planners (in which buses, assigned to special lanes, could control traffic lights)...

*Select the combination that works best in the preceding context.*_____

Now create a similar set of simple sentences from the words printed in bold type and combine the simple sentences in the ways shown in the model. On line d, add your own combination. Then select the one that best fits the given context.

1

CONTEXT:
In the early nineteenth century, little was known by most white Americans about Native American life and customs. In the hope of creating a more sympathetic view of this continent's original residents, **George Catlin painted portraits; the Native Americans that were in these portraits were portrayed with dignity, and they also looked proudly upon their viewers.** Many of these portraits may be found today in the Catlin Gallery of the National Museum in Washington, D.C.

SIMPLE SENTENCES:
1. _____
2. _____
3. _____
4. _____

RECOMBINATIONS:
(a) _____
(b) _____
(c) _____
(d) _____

*Select the combination that works best in the preceding context.*_____

2

CONTEXT:
Prose is not the only format for social commentary. **Songs are written by modern folksingers, and in these songs serious issues are treated in a satirical way and are brought to public attention,** and editorial cartoons drawn by a new generation of artists (in which any person or policy can easily be made to look ridiculous) are quite effective in influencing public opinion.

SIMPLE SENTENCES:
1. _____
2. _____
3. _____
4. _____

RECOMBINATIONS:
(a) _____
(b) _____
(c) _____
(d) _____

Select the combination that works best in the preceding context._____

3

CONTEXT:
Georges Méliès was a professional magician, and he quickly realized how the tricks of his trade could be applied to the brand-new medium of motion pictures. **Méliès made films, photographing actors with primitive equipment, and in these films the actors were able to disappear, change size, and fly through the air** as early as 1897. Audiences at the time were amazed and truly frightened by these effects.

SIMPLE SENTENCES:
1. _____
2. _____
3. _____
4. _____

RECOMBINATIONS:

(a) _____

(b) _____

(c) _____

(d) _____

Select the combination that works best in the preceding context. _____

OPEN EXERCISE A

The following is a draft of a short essay. The sentences printed in bold type are similar to those you worked with in the previous exercise. Revise these sentences so that they work well in the context of the essay. Compare your solutions with those of your classmates and be prepared to discuss the choices you have made.

Two Approaches to Acting

The primary task of an actor is to create a believable character. Two very different techniques for accomplishing this task have evolved over the years: the first might be called "working from the inside"; the second, "working from the outside." **Drawing from their own acting experience, the instructors in classes that many drama students attend teach either one technique or the other to drama students in classes.** Only seldom do students receive training in both approaches to acting.

"Working from the inside" is another name for what is more popularly known as Method acting. Actors who use this technique try to find parallels between their own lives and those of the characters they play. **Classes in Method acting often include improvisational exercises in which the actors, without scripts and without pre-written plots, must create characters that seem real and must create scenes that seem real.** By feeling the feelings and thinking the thoughts that their characters feel and think, Method actors find that they can more naturally behave the way their characters would behave.

"Working from the outside" is a technique used quite often by actors trained in repertory companies. Called upon to play a great variety of different characters, these actors have found observation to be their most valuable tool. **They often visit places in which there are different types of people, and these people, who are of all ages and all backgrounds, can be watched and studied.** These actors concentrate on the physical mannerisms of the people they see: ways of moving, of talking, and of reacting. By selecting and using the outward characteristics that seem appropriate, an actor who "works from the outside" can build a complete, believable character out of a collection of small details.

MODELED EXERCISE B

CONTEXT:
Most people think of their shoes as containing only "natural" materials. In reality, **the chemicals that many manufacturers use to make shoes are not uncommon causes of allergic reactions** that can produce excessive foot odor. Some shoe companies in the United States manufacture shoes that will not cause allergic reactions; a foot doctor can provide their addresses.

SIMPLE SENTENCES:
1. Many manufacturers use chemicals to make shoes.
2. These chemicals are causes of allergic reactions.
3. The causes are common.

RECOMBINATIONS:
(a) The chemicals that many manufacturers use to make shoes are common causes of allergic reactions.
(b) Many manufacturers use chemicals to make shoes, and these chemicals are common causes of allergic reactions.
(c) Common causes of allergic reactions are the chemicals that many manufacturers use to make shoes.

Select the combination that works best in the preceding context._____

Now create a similar set of simple sentences from the words printed in bold type and combine the simple sentences in the ways shown in the model. On line d, add your own combination. Then select the one that best fits the given context.

1

CONTEXT:
It has become increasingly clear over the past 30 years that **the fictional situations that George Orwell created in his book** *Nineteen Eighty-Four* **may not be unrealistic predictions of our own world's future.** For example, Orwell's fictional world is divided into three superstates called Oceania, Eurasia, and Eastasia. In the 1980s, global influence is similarly divided among three great superpowers—the United States, the Soviet Union, and the People's Republic of China.

SIMPLE SENTENCES:
1. _____
2. _____
3. _____

RECOMBINATIONS:
(a) _____
(b) _____
(c) _____
(d) _____

Select the combination that works best in the preceding context. _____

2

CONTEXT:
The German astronomer Johannes Kepler had suffered from a childhood disease that left him with very poor eyesight. Therefore, he was unable to make any direct observations of the universe. Instead, **the mathematical skills that Kepler applied to other astronomers' observations were sufficient to win him a not unimportant place in scientific history.** Kepler's calculations resulted in simple mathematical formulas that were able to account for all the complex movements of the planets.

SIMPLE SENTENCES:
1. _____
2. _____
3. _____

RECOMBINATIONS:
(a) _____
(b) _____
(c) _____
(d) _____

Select the combination that works best in the preceding context._____

3

CONTEXT:
Human beings have always craved salt; in fact, salt is a necessary part of every mammal's diet. In ancient Rome, where pure salt was a rarity because there were few developed salt mines, **salt that the Romans had pressed into bars was not an unusual form of payment for soldiers.** The modern phrase "worth one's salt" can be traced back to this practice.

SIMPLE SENTENCES:
1. _____
2. _____
3. _____

RECOMBINATIONS:
(a) _____
(b) _____
(c) _____
(d) _____

Select the combination that works best in the preceding context._____

OPEN EXERCISE B

The following is a draft of a short essay. The sentences printed in bold type are similar to those you worked with in the previous exercise. Revise these sentences so that they work well in the context of the essay. Compare your solutions with those of your classmates and be prepared to discuss the choices you have made.

Spreading the Light

The revolution that **Helen Keller brought about in the lives of the handicapped was not an unremarkable accomplishment**—especially since Keller was both blind and deaf. Left unable to see or hear after an illness she had suffered as an infant, Keller soon forgot the few words she knew and became mute as well. Because she had to communicate nonverbally to get what she wanted, her frustration with people who did not understand her quickly led to tantrums. Her family took such behavior for granted, since both blind and deaf people in the late 1800s were still classified as idiots. However, on the advice of Alexander Graham Bell, a noted teacher of the deaf, Keller's parents sent for a teacher from the Perkins Institution for the Blind.

Shortly thereafter, in 1887, Anne Sullivan—a nineteen-year-old orphan—arrived from Boston at the Kellers' house. Thus began a relationship that would last until Sullivan's death and would show what a loving teacher can do with a deaf and blind pupil. By means of a manual alphabet, Sullivan spelled words into Keller's hand. Frustrating as it was, **the responsibility of educating Keller did not turn out to be an unrewarding task.** Once Keller finally realized that everything had its own special name, she progressed rapidly. By 1900, Keller was ready to enroll at Radcliffe College, where Sullivan "spelled" the lectures into the young student's hand.

Keller graduated from Radcliffe College *cum laude* and soon received worldwide acclaim. **Her decision to devote her life to helping blind and deaf people was not a cowardly choice.** Before that time, public discussion of deaf and blind people had been taboo because of the supposed connection between these disabilities and venereal disease. Keller, through her essays and articles, succeeded in opening the columns of major magazines and newspapers to the subject of handicapped people. She made the country aware of its responsibilities to the afflicted. By 1937, thirty states had established commissions for the blind. Not only was Keller able to expand the limits of her own world, but she was able to shed light on the dark worlds of other handicapped people as well.

MODELED EXERCISE C

CONTEXT:
Some animals find their prey by sensing heat. **Two heat-sensing pits that are beneath its eyes are used by a rattlesnake to locate warm-blooded prey.** A mosquito flies toward any warm surface, while a blood-sucking tick responds to an increase in the temperature of its front legs.

SIMPLE SENTENCES:
1. A rattlesnake locates warm-blooded prey.
2. It uses two heat-sensing pits to do this.
3. The pits are beneath its eyes.

RECOMBINATIONS:
(a) A rattlesnake locates warm-blooded prey by using two heat-sensing pits that are beneath its eyes.
(b) Using two heat-sensing pits that are beneath its eyes, a rattlesnake locates warm-blooded prey.
(c) To locate warm-blooded prey, a rattlesnake uses two heat-sensing pits that are beneath its eyes.

*Select the combination that works best in the preceding context.*_____

Now create a similar set of simple sentences from the words printed in bold type and combine the simple sentences in the ways shown in the model. On line d, add your own combination. Then select the one that best fits the given context.

1

CONTEXT:
Because wood and iron were unavailable, the Polar Eskimos of Greenland made good use of meteorites. **In order to make hunting tools, blades were shaped by the Eskimos out of metal that had fallen from space thousands of years before.** Many of these tools and some of the ancient meteorites themselves were found by the explorer Robert E. Peary. Transporting them to New York City was a task that took four Arctic summers.

SIMPLE SENTENCES:
1. _____
2. _____
3. _____

RECOMBINATIONS:
(a) _____
(b) _____
(c) _____
(d) _____

*Select the combination that works best in the preceding context.*_____

2

CONTEXT:
After the Great Fire of 1666 destroyed three-quarters of the city, Sir Christopher Wren, the greatest architect of his time, designed 52 London churches. **A dome that dominated the skyline of London was added by Wren to crown his masterpiece, St. Paul's Cathedral.** Its grace and simplicity contrast with the intricate decorative details of the cathedral itself.

SIMPLE SENTENCES:
1. _____
2. _____
3. _____

RECOMBINATIONS:
(a) _____
(b) _____
(c) _____
(d) _____

*Select the combination that works best in the preceding context.*_____

3

CONTEXT:
The alpine winter's deep snow causes few problems for the woodland caribou. **Wide hooves that are equipped with long dewclaws can be used by the caribou to find food under the snow.** The caribou can find food *above* the snow as well: standing atop a heavy layer of snow, it can reach lichens on high tree branches.

SIMPLE SENTENCES:
1. _____
2. _____
3. _____

RECOMBINATIONS:
(a) _____
(b) _____
(c) _____
(d) _____

Select the combination that works best in the preceding context._____

OPEN EXERCISE C

The following is a draft of a short essay. The sentences printed in bold type are similar to those you worked with in the previous exercise. Revise these sentences so that they work well in the context of the essay. Compare your solutions with those of your classmates and be prepared to discuss the choices you have made.

Eleanor Roosevelt: First Lady of the World

Eleanor Roosevelt is widely regarded as the most admired and most important first lady the United States has had. **Her husband, President Franklin Delano Roosevelt, was influenced by her bringing of attention to the widespread poverty that existed in the country.** Because FDR had been crippled by polio, Mrs. Roosevelt traveled extensively as his representative. She circled the globe several times, visiting military bases during World War II and meeting most of the world's leaders.

A daily newspaper column that was read throughout the country was written by Mrs. Roosevelt to make her own opinions known. Her humanitarian views influenced national policy toward young people, blacks, women and the poor. Such issues as child welfare, slum clearance and equal rights were important to her.

After FDR's death, Eleanor Roosevelt thought that her life as a public figure was over. Instead, President Harry S. Truman asked her to serve as a delegate to the United Nations. The other members of her delegation questioned her qualifications, but she soon proved to be an effective leader. **A U.N. commission that worked for human rights was headed by her in order to benefit people all over the world.** Indeed, Eleanor Roosevelt's courageous support for the rights of individuals throughout her public life made her the true conscience of the nation and earned her the title "First Lady of the World."

MODELED EXERCISE D

CONTEXT:
Although the squirrel's tail cannot grasp tree branches (as the tails of many monkeys can), it nevertheless helps the squirrel move quickly from place to place. **The squirrel leaps through the air, and it uses its tail as a rudder to control the angle of its fall;** dropping to the ground, it uses its tail as a brake or a parachute.

SIMPLE SENTENCES:
1. The squirrel leaps through the air.
2. It uses its tail as a rudder.
3. It does this to change the angle of its fall.

RECOMBINATIONS:
(a) Leaping through the air, the squirrel uses its tail as a rudder to change the angle of its fall.
(b) Using its tail as a rudder to change the angle of its fall, the squirrel leaps through the air.
(c) Leaping through the air, the squirrel changes the angle of its fall by using its tail as a rudder.

Select the combination that works best in the preceding context._____

Now create a similar set of simple sentences from the words printed in bold type and combine the simple sentences in the ways shown in the model. On line d, add your own combination. Then select the one that best fits the given context.

1

CONTEXT:
Betty Friedan sensed that something was wrong in women's lives, and, to try to define the problem, she wrote *The Feminine Mystique* in the early 1960s. The book forced many people to re-evaluate the role that women had played in society and helped to bring about the movement that became known as "women's liberation."

SIMPLE SENTENCES:
1. _____
2. _____
3. _____

RECOMBINATIONS:
(a) _____
(b) _____
(c) _____
(d) _____

Select the combination that works best in the preceding context._____

2

CONTEXT:
Hundreds of carrion beetles work as museum employees; they strip the flesh from animals to clean the skeletons for display in Yale University's natural history museum. The insects are rewarded with deluxe accommodations in the museum's basement.

SIMPLE SENTENCES:
1. _____
2. _____
3. _____

RECOMBINATIONS:
(a) _____
(b) _____

(c) _____

(d) _____

Select the combination that works best in the preceding context._____

3

CONTEXT:

Perhaps because of the modern-day society that bears his name, John James Audubon is often thought of as a conservationist. On the contrary, Audubon was primarily an artist—and sometimes, for the sake of his art, he found it necessary to shoot the birds and animals he intended to draw. **Audubon sometimes used dozens of freshly killed models to complete one painting, and he achieved a realism that was unprecedented in wildlife illustration.** Nevertheless, scientists later criticized Audubon for having painted some of his animals in poses that they would never assume in real life.

SIMPLE SENTENCES:

1. _____

2. _____

3. _____

RECOMBINATIONS:

(a) _____

(b) _____

(c) _____

(d) _____

Select the combination that works best in the preceding context._____

OPEN EXERCISE D

The following is a draft of a short essay. The sentences printed in bold type are similar to those you worked with in the previous exercise. Revise these sentences so that they work well in the context of the essay. Compare your solutions with those of your classmates and be prepared to discuss the choices you have made.

Beauty in Bits and Pieces

Stained glass is nothing more than ordinary glass that has been colored with metal oxides. However, once it has been cut into pieces and reassembled with strips of lead, stained glass can take on an unearthly brilliance. Artists discovered centuries ago that their mosaics of colored glass were most effective when brightly lit from behind; thus it is not surprising that stained glass has almost always been used to make windows.

Medieval architects borrowed technology from the Middle East; they began to use primitive stained-glass panels to enhance the beauty of their churches. Not only did stained-glass windows induce a spiritual atmosphere; they also offered a religious education to the often illiterate churchgoers by illustrating Biblical scenes and figures. The earliest stained-glass windows still in existence are five glass panels in the cathedral of Augsburg, Germany. **These panels date from the eleventh century, and they use simple shapes and colors to depict five Biblical prophets.** Stained-glass windows became more complex in the twelfth and thirteenth centuries, but their great expense made it impossible for any but the most elaborate cathedrals to afford them.

In the fourteenth century, however, it was discovered that glass coated with silver nitrate would turn yellow when fired in an oven. This process, because it was so inexpensive, made stained glass available to many more churches. Unfortunately, it was at about this time that stained glass began its decline as an art form. By the fifteenth century, artists were simply painting designs onto pieces of clear glass rather than building mosaics out of colored glass shapes. Eventually, by the seventeenth century, the art of making true stained glass had been virtually forgotten.

It was not until the late nineteenth century that artists in Europe and the United States spurred a revived interest in stained glass. While some artists tried to imitate the great windows of the twelfth and thirteenth centuries, others sought to find a more modern way to use this ancient technique. One such artist who is still admired today is Louis Comfort Tiffany. **Tiffany worked around the turn of the century, and he used brightly colored stained glass to make such practical objects as vases and lampshades.**

Today, the creation of stained glass remains an imaginative, highly developed art. Many artists, such as Marc Chagall, have designed beautiful stained-glass windows for modern religious structures. In addition, people have developed new techniques for working with stained glass. (For example, many stained-glass windows are now held together with epoxy rather than lead.) Even after hundreds of years, stained glass retains its power to thrill and inspire those who enter into its light.

———— • ————

The stained-glass panel on the cover of this book was designed and executed by Leslie Pfahl. It was photographed by Tom Dunham.

ABOUT THE AUTHORS

John Clifford is an Assistant Professor of English at the University of North Carolina at Wilmington. He is on the editorial board for *Composition and Teaching.* During the academic year 1980–81 he was an NEH Fellow-in-Residence for Literature in Literacy at the University of Southern California, and he attended the NDEA Seminar for Chairmen in Composition and Linguistics, Drake University, 1968. Dr. Clifford's publications include the Instructor's Manual for *The Random House Guide to Writing, Modern American Prose* (Random House, 1983), and numerous papers and articles on composition for such academic journals as *Research in the Teaching of English, College English,* and *College Composition and Communication.* He was a consultant for Daiker, Kerek and Morenberg's *A Writer's Options* (Harper & Row) and also for the *Random House Handbook* and the *Random House Reader.* He has a Ph.D. from New York University.

Robert F. Waterhouse is editorial director of Visual Education Corporation, an editorial development company in Princeton, N.J. He has a B.A. in Classical Languages and in English Language and Literature from Oxford University, England, and an M.A. in Communications from the University of Pennsylvania in Philadelphia. As editorial director he has developed educational programs and textbooks in English and other subjects, both at the high school and at the college level. He has also lectured in English and Communications at Trenton State College, Trenton, N.J.